The Varied Origins of the Cyber Men

Compiled by

Lisa Ventura

Copyright Notice

Copyright © 2020: UKCSA Publications (part of the UK Cyber Security Association).

Publisher: UKCSA Publications (part of UK Cyber Sec Assoc Ltd, a company registered in England and Wales no 11903684.)
The moral rights of the authors have been asserted.

All rights reserved. No part of this publication may be reproduced or distributed in any form or by any means, including photocopying, recording or other electronic or mechanical methods, without the prior written permission of the publisher, except in the case of brief quotation embodied in critical reviews and certain other non-commercial uses permitted by copyright law. For permission request, please write to:

Lisa Ventura
Editor: The Varied Origins of the Cyber Men
UK Cyber Sec Assoc Ltd, 1 King Street, Worcester, WR1 2NX.
Tel: 0800 772 0155
Email: info@cybersecurityassociation.co.uk
Web: www.cybersecurityassociation.co.uk

Contents **Page**

Introduction by Tyler Cohen Wood

Disclaimer

Acknowledgements and Thanks

Chapter 1   Adrian Taylor

Chapter 2   Chris Windley

Chapter 3   Ciaran Durnin

Chapter 4   James Bore

Chapter 5   Mark Shawa

Chapter 6   Nathan Chung

Chapter 7   Nathaniel Schooler

Chapter 8   Phillip Winstanley

Chapter 9   Rory Innes

Chapter 10   Tim Burnett

Coming in November 2021 – The Varied Origins of the Cyber Men: Volume 2

Introduction by Tyler Cohen Wood

TO BE PROVIDED BY TYLER COHEN WOOD.

Disclaimer

The chapters in this book have been submitted by those featured. As such the writing style of each chapter has been kept as far as possible particularly with regard to culture, language, terminology and how the chapters are constructed. The chapters are a mix of first person and third person accounts, and American spellings have been retained in some of them where appropriate.

Each chapter is unique to the writer and the Editor did not want to change the essence of the chapters submitted, although the book has been proofread by the Editor and a third party for clarity.

All chapters have been approved and signed off by the individual contributors.

Acknowledgements and Thanks

My sincere thanks go to everyone included in this book for taking the time to write and submit their chapters for inclusion. I also express my thanks to all the men in cyber security all over the world who we have interacted with in the course of compiling this book and for their insights, hints, tips and more to help others who are considering a career in the cyber security industry. You have all inspired me to do more, be better and to achieve more.

Thanks also go to Gill Tolley of AssignIt2Me for proofreading this book, and to my husband Russell Ventura for his unwavering support.

Finally, I would like to extend my sincere thanks to everyone in the Infosec community on social media, particularly on Twitter and LinkedIn, who I have got to know and who have supported me with this project. You know who you all are.

Lisa Ventura
Editor: The Varied Origins of the Cyber Men

Chapter 1

Name: Adrian Taylor
Job Title: Strategy Hacker & Coach
Company: Bluecap Solutions Ltd
Location: Bristol, UK

I was sitting there on one of the most beautiful beaches in Thailand as I pushed my laptop to the side so I could drink the contents of my fresh coconut and watch the sun go down over the horizon.

The day had been researching how to work through imposter syndrome for my leadership coaching qualification. It was fascinating to me. I was reading about people who even though they had a wealth of experience and skills, were crippled by the fear that one day they'd be found out. They typically spent their days feeling they were frauds which led either to being total perfectionists and workaholics, or to step behind their fears and out of what their potential was.

I had an assignment to complete and part of that was to write my 'coaching profile' describing the kind of coach I was and why I could help people. I'd been putting it off for ages, as I really didn't feel I had anything to offer the industry.

And there it was, the realisation. As the sun set and I chewed my bamboo straw, it struck me, like a coconut from a tree - I was one of the people I was reading about, I was a massive imposter in the cyber security world.

That was ten months ago actually, in February 2020. I had to smile wryly at the irony of the situation! There I was, two months into an over-winter trip through Asia, house rented out and balancing a part-time cyber security contract, whilst spending the rest of my time studying coaching, mindfulness, and yoga. I was living the dream, my dream. However, I did not believe it was real, it would surely be taken away at any point.

Enough was enough, I did some breathing exercises, had another coconut (or probably a beer!) and decided to go through my own notes and do some self-coaching!

One of the exercises suggested taking time to write my story and highlight my achievements along the way.

So, here is the story I did everything in my power to avoid writing, the one I didn't think was exciting enough to write. The story of a biologist who found his way to work for one of the best incident response companies in the world and then go on to wear a suit or yoga gear with equal comfort.

Where to begin? Let me take you right back to when I was about 7 and sitting outside my back door with a broken toy helicopter in one hand and a hammer in the other. I wanted to fix it, but more than anything I REALLY needed to find out how it worked. The chances of fixing it with a hammer were pretty slim, but I gave it a good go. As I began to bash it open, I started to see how the different cogs fitted together and how moving one bit over here would make the rotors move over there. I was fascinated.

A week later, I was sitting in the doctor's surgery because I was having some breathing issues in one of my nostrils. The doctor was having a good old poke around and then with a tug on his tweezers he pulled out a lump of red plastic from my nose. It was actually a piece of the helicopter I was bashing with a hammer the week before. It must have shot right up my nose and stayed undetected all that time. Fascinating! Where did it go? How did the body work? I didn't stop asking questions from that point on. I was hooked on finding out how things worked and most of my toys ended up being either toolsets, transformers, or Lego.

I grew up on the rural coast of Essex. My dad was a chronic workaholic, owning a business selling speedboats & water-skis. It always sounds idyllic when I tell people this and likely conjures up images of me constantly playing on boats and being on the water learning to ski. The frustrating reality though was my dad worked 6.5 days a week and my mum often had to work alongside him. He worked far too hard and on his time off the last thing he wanted to do was take out boats for fun.

In fact, the closest I got to the boats was being paid pocket money to wash them, or sitting in them, whilst his mechanic fixed the broken ones. The mechanic must have had the patience of a saint to be fair. He was there, trying to fix engines and there was I, a young boy relentlessly asking, "what's that then?", "what's that do?", "can I help", every few seconds.

As I grew up, if I wasn't washing boats or playing with friends down on the beach, I had my nose in David Attenborough books or documentaries. Not surprisingly, I ended up loving science at school. I was curious about computers at the time, but it was the early nineties and in that prehistoric age, I would have needed to travel to another town to pursue them at A-levels. I chose biology, so I could be closer to my friends.

I was a spotty kid, with some shocking curtains and braces that gave me a lisp. I was super lanky, had two left feet and was probably 6 foot by the time I was 13. Kids are cruel and bullied me mercilessly as I was different in so many ways.

It was survival of the fittest and I was far from the fittest! I had to find a different way out and I learnt not to be the victim, but to observe, notice and then adapt. I was never going to be the cool kid, but I would find my way through. Oh, and when I stopped being so lanky, just big, that helped too!

I read books on body language, human instinct, and nature vs nurture. I learnt to listen to what was really happening around me and was fascinated by what people were telling me with their bodies, but not by their mouths. I could tell a liar or someone hiding the truth a mile away.

Growing these skills had an interesting impact, people felt listened to and they became super comfortable telling me things they wouldn't tell others.

At that time, my first job was in a nursing home, where the residents would happily tell their tales to a curious young whippersnapper. Saying that, so would the other nurses and carers and a young teenager sure learnt a lot in those years!

Anyway, I digress. Let me take you forward to university in Swansea where I became an Environmental Biology student. I learnt the skills of a scientist - to be curious about everything but do it in a structured way so you can prove or disprove a theory.

I was a shocking student, easily distracted away from most things other than animal behaviour and ecology. I didn't appreciate it as a skill at the time, but I was great at seeing the interrelationships between things and their environment.

Blimey, I think I just paid my younger self a compliment there. This coaching exercise must be working!

I had a rubbish dissertation topic though. When I say that, I genuinely did, I analysed bat droppings for weeks. I laid them out in tubs and then dissolved them overnight before looking at them down the microscope for anything of interest like an insect's jaw or knee that would tell me what it had eaten.

It's a bit like sitting through many vendor presentations; you're just waiting for the slides to dissolve away until you get to the bits you really want to know!

Little did I know at that point, that later in life I would go full circle and make a career out of spotting bat shit or looking for interesting things in logs!

I wasn't one for working so much in labs though and decided that I'd stick with my BSc and go explore other options.

I hadn't a clue what I was going to do though and picked an IT recruitment job out the back of the paper. I used computers in my degree, so it was obviously a perfect fit!

I didn't like the job too much but was super interested in the money people were making out of IT, it was much better than biology. I used my time to learn about all the types of IT jobs and how candidates progressed in their careers. I started to map out what paths needed qualifications or super technical skills, and which didn't. Not having a qualification wasn't a barrier as long as I was willing to use a bit of initiative and start at the bottom. IT support desk, here I come!

I wrote down the names of about 50 hiring managers in Cardiff and took a day off to phone them all up until one of them gave me a job. I got a job on a bank's service desk and answered about 300 calls a day, anything from a broken mouse to Lotus Notes servers crashing. I learnt to incident manage and the value of keeping a clear head and dealing in facts until a pattern emerged which would help diagnose the issues.

I was only a few months in and was working the late shift on 9/11. Our bank had a massive New York office and several hundred working in the WT7 building. Their building wasn't struck by a plane that day, but the structural damage of the other buildings falling meant it fully collapsed later that night. My UK technical colleagues all tried to divert critical operations, without knowing whether any of their UK teammates were alive. It was very humbling to support where I could that day, fielding calls from very confused and scared people. My colleagues all escaped with their lives that day. I will never forget that shift and the impact it had on us all in the weeks to come. It was there that I had my first experience of working on a major incident and realised the true importance of teamwork, compassion, and solid communication.

The job ended when our roles were outsourced to India. I was contracting and I remember asking the Security Manager if I could get a job in his team, rather than have to leave. Sadly, he didn't think I had the right experience or qualifications to get into security at that time. I had to wait a little longer.

I was bored as we ramped down, so whilst my boss was on leave I decided to re-write all the training guides ready for the Indian team to pick up the mantle. They looked pretty and I was super excited to show my boss this when she returned. I thought it would be a nice surprise because "the old one was a bit light on the ground and could definitely be modernised". Wow, if looks could kill! I nearly turned to stone as she asked, very unimpressed "and what specifically was wrong with the ones I did?". Whoops!

Oh well, I left the bank with a copy of the very glossy training guides in hand and got a job as a technical author & trainer at Sony, helping them document and train their customers on a lean manufacturing tool which optimised throughput. I learned so much in this job.

It taught me the value of doing things right, first time. On a factory line if someone put the wrong resistor in a TV it could blow up in someone's house, potentially costing life, or at the very least a costly and embarrassing recall. Putting in adequate quality checks prevented costly slips and meant teams focused on production and not re-working. A valuable lesson. It also taught me first-hand many of the concepts I read about much later in "The Phoenix Project". A shame I didn't write it though, it's done rather well!

The job took me to far-flung lands from the start. Eight weeks in, I had to run a course in Malaysia. The only problem was I had totally exaggerated my interview when I said I was an experienced IT trainer! Oh well, it was time to buy 'The IT Trainers Toolkit for Beginners' book and cram.

I loved the experience of working overseas in Mexico, China, Hong Kong, Eastern Europe, and the USA. I always tried to live like the locals and whilst my hosts would want to take me to the standard American style restaurants frequented by other visitors, I would ask to eat at local cafes and street stalls.

I was overseas for a month at a time with a couple of developers for company; it was great fun! We would work ridiculously long hours during the week, deploying and debugging the logs of (really) buggy software. On the weekends, we'd play as hard as we could in far flung lands. I went on to have a great few years in Sony and matured from young, green rookie trainer to Customer Success Manager and Project Manager. I must have travelled to about 20 countries and it really ignited my passion for experiencing the world.

I loved the travel that took a leap of faith and quit the 'proper job' to head off with a backpack for a nine-month trip around the world. I didn't regret it one minute. It was glorious and such a formative trip for me. I discovered meditation and yoga in Asia and learnt to trust my instincts more whilst exploring jungles in South America.
I even spent a couple of weeks on a silent retreat in a monastery deep inside a Thai jungle. It was a bit like that scene in The Dark Knight where Bruce Wayne ends up training in the Himalayas, only this place was much sweatier and more yoga and meditation than martial arts!

Nevertheless, like all good things, I had to come back, and was lucky enough to find a contract as a Service Delivery manager… the job that truly set me up for my security career.

I found myself sitting in between technical stakeholders, developers, and customers. I was again in effect a connector or a translator. I would coordinate large incidents, build stakeholder confidence and be the person who people called to find out why their (newsworthy) website went down!

After a while I was called the "shit filter" because I was the person wheeled out when engineers messed up. That wore thin after a while and I needed a change.

Luckily, an ex-techie colleague of mine was working for a defence company who needed someone who knew services to help set up a Security Operations Centre aka SOC. It was time to take a leap.

I was an ITIL obsessed, service delivery manager and a few days after handing in my notice, I was sitting across the office from a recently hired and very pragmatic senior leader in the organisation. A part of me was hoping he was going to convince me to stay and offer me the long overdue pay rise and more responsibility. But instead, he was perhaps the most honest anyone had been to me in years - he shared his view of the organisation and let me know that nothing he could offer me would give as great a challenge as that which awaited me…. in security!

But his next question was perhaps the most helpful, enlightening and frightening - "did I have any idea how big a step I was taking?" Well no, I had absolutely no clue, but during the next hour of conversation he helped me feel ready to take a leap of faith and 'get into security'. Ok, after 10 years of designing, building, and running security operations 'stuff' I always tell people the biggest lesson I ever learnt was over-reliance on technology and under investment on the people. I learnt that lesson in this job.

At the time we had an "insert appropriate collective noun" for wonderfully helpful yet hands-off 'consultants' who were buzzing around carrying large documents to be reviewed. Not one of them could configure a SIEM or prioritise threat scenarios to be monitored.

So, I did what any young, ambitious, and curious soul would do - I got that hammer out again and started hitting the books until I worked out how things worked. I remember reading the 2011 copy of the Mandiant M-Trends report when it came out and the APT-1 report. They were amazing and I was hooked! It is funny, it is 10 years on but I'm still explaining to clients what clicked for me that year: Logs + Network visibility + Endpoint visibility = almost a cat's chance in hell at finding something. Mandiant were awesome in my eyes and I only dreamed of working with them one day as they just seemed to be so far ahead of everyone else.

I learnt so much in that time, mainly how not to do things to be honest, but learning all the same! I learnt the value of hiring a diverse team and mixing experienced members with fresh young ideas and attitude. I was too process heavy to begin with (blame ITIL), but soon learnt that to keep up with the curve I had to find a space for people to explore and experiment in order to find new ways of doing things.

I learnt the value of agility in teams and focussing on small, incremental wins over talk about boiling oceans. It was a super-steep learning curve, but I was lapping it up and loving every long day I worked.

I took my knowledge into my first consulting gig, where I helped a large systems integrator front some of their cyber security projects into their clients. Somehow, in just a few years I found myself as a cyber tech lead, designing massive operations capabilities and building blueprints of next gen capabilities alongside Microsoft and two of the big four. I even got my chance to work alongside Mandiant a couple of times. My heroes!

I can see the thread again - I was working once more as the glue between many specialists and business stakeholders. I would one minute be rolling my sleeves up in the detail and the next lifting out of it to help people connect the dots and build a vision and strategy. I was never far from a whiteboard and often found waving my hands around as I built up the picture of what we wanted to achieve.
It was good fun, and there came a time when I was hungering to be in a room full of ridiculously bright cyber people with whom I could learn even more.

Around that time, one of the folks I knew from Mandiant said they were looking to hire their second ever tech specialist on the ground in the UK and he thought I'd be a good fit. The conversation was a little like "Mandiant? Really? Me? No! There is no way. These people are insanely bright… Ah, go on then…. I may as well interview."

Blimey, that was the most intense interview experience of my entire life. They gave me a forensic package (Redline) from a compromised host and said I needed to give a presentation of my findings to the global head of engineering in two days' time. I was well over my head. I was the team and processes guy.

I nearly threw in the towel, but I really wanted this chance and decided to learn forensics as I went. I literally went through this forensic package line by line, looking up everything on google from the meaning of the specific registry keys, process arguments and system log messages.

There were thousands of lines in the logs but slowly a pattern emerged, and I was excited to piece together an attack.
Holy shit, I got the job! I was employed by Mandiant and being flown over to their HQ to be trained! It was an amazing experience! For the next few years, I kept finding opportunities to feel the newbie in the room and learn from the best malware, intelligence, and incident response experts in the industry. I think Mandiant were the pioneers of EDR & MDR and I was lucky enough to work with them and their customers as the business grew across the globe. I went on to support their Global Accounts and got to play geek in a tonne of more fun places around the world.

It was a great culture that thrived because people enjoyed the challenge and would help each other solve whatever was in front of them. I learnt again the value of diversity. Everyone had their different backgrounds, capabilities, and personalities; it was only when each of these differences were given a chance to shine did the fun stuff happen.

It was probably then when things started to shift for me. I became less hungry to solve things myself and was more inclined to work with others to build things that would last. I started to drop the ego a bit and realised that lifestyle and balance was much more important to me than targets and OKRs! I obviously loved exploring the world with my camera and it was time to listen to those itchy feet and head off into the sunset with my backpack once more.

I took 10 months out to travel from Mexico down through to Ecuador and ended up in the Galapagos Islands, fulfilling my dream to follow in the footsteps of Darwin. I was so grateful for the fun, adventures, and random experiences along the way (except perhaps for waking up with a scorpion on my pillow). I surf boarded down the outside of an active volcano, paddled down the amazon, dived with whale sharks, turtles and penguins and lived on an island in the middle of a volcanic lake.

I learnt the gift of trusting my instincts and truly tuning into what I wanted to do in life, not where others were pointing me. Again, I deepened my studies of mindfulness and yoga and spent a huge amount of time with local cultures that had wonderfully close-knit communities at the heart of their successes.

I felt truly happy in these travels, but also knew I needed to work to sustain this balance. I didn't want to return to another permanent job and have to beg to take time off to travel. Therefore, I decided that contracting was my only option, helping others with their cyber security challenges, whilst being very honest that I was only going to be there to help them architect and build their capabilities, before handing them over to teams to run them.

I'm almost at the end of my story, but there is one other lesson I learnt along the way, that has brought me to where I am now, the value of openness, vulnerability, community, and culture.

This happened not in the office, but outside of it, when in Nicaragua. I was living in a community there where people each day, before they went to work, would sit in a circle, and share what was going on for them. Anything was welcome and it was a hugely emotional and inspirational process to be part of. The courage people had when they shared their feelings with such openness and vulnerability was amazing. Because everyone was a part of this 'circle' the community stayed strong and supportive. When one person was low, the others were there to offer support when needed.

I started to realise that even though I was good at connecting people I had been prone to 'tunnelling' where I would grab hold of a challenge and get my head down to design and build a solution on my own. I realised that just like when I raced off and re-wrote that training manual, I was still prone to running off on my own all these years later. Instead, I needed more 'team' and community in the change projects I ran.

Tunnelling was not great for a change leader because instead of the cheers and champagne when I walked in with a massive solutions doc in my hand, I would be met with blank looks and folks not reading beyond the first few pages.

I had thought up the solution, but often they hadn't even started to understand the problem. This was always really rubbish and I would feel disconnected, demotivated, underappreciated, and normally pretty frustrated.

I started to look back at past successes and failures and see that the pattern to more successful projects was always when I got people's buy-in earlier. Yes, people wanted me to help on those challenges, but they didn't want me to run off as an SME and just solve it, they wanted to be part of that process and come on that journey too.
I have to admit that I do enjoy getting the music cranked up and hacking my way through a challenge, but there's nothing as fulfilling

these days as solving problems within a diverse team of people and seeing us all grow together as a result.

I now make sure I remember to think of 'people over project', and 'progress over perfection'.

Here is where I have found my home in cyber security. In the last couple of years, I have been bringing together my love of travel and independence with my love of cyber security and of bringing people together to overcome challenges.

I have invested heavily in training myself in coaching and transformative leadership, as well as yoga and mindfulness. All of these come together and help me live a more authentic, open life where I can help others grow and flourish.

A couple of years back I set up a small consulting company called Bluecap. The name fits for a couple of reasons, firstly I'm a blue teamer, but more importantly a Bluecap is a mythical flame creature that lives in tunnels & mines. It helps those lost or in danger by shining its blue light and showing them the way to safety.

That's my mission - I help leaders, teams and organisations navigate their own way through the dangerous mines I've become familiar with all these years. I help break down silos in organisations and bring security teams closer to the businesses they're protecting.

I do this through coaching, running creative problem-solving workshops, or rolling my sleeves up in complex projects. Together we find the tools, people and ways that are necessary to protect organisations.

I smile when I read this because I'm just like that little kid with the toy helicopter. When I see something's not working well I just can't walk past it, I have to open it up and see how all the pieces fit together. I may not use a hammer to get things working these days, but in my toolbox of coaching and problem solving I help people hack their strategies into byte-sized, achievable chunks.

But what about that imposter syndrome? Oh yeah! It sucks! I often have to dig deep to truly believe that I have anything useful to share with others. It's kicked in as I wrote this! I found every excuse under the sun to avoid pressing send! My 'inner critic' voice is screaming at me not to bother, there'll be someone else far more interesting to go into the book!

I tell that voice to STFU and instead I pay way more attention to my 'inner coach' voice that helps me bring in the resources I need to step up.

That coaching article I was reading ... whilst on the beach in Thailand, on my third 6 month sabbatical, studying yoga, running my own company and successfully coaching people remotely ... was right, it really does help to write things down and reflect on them. I can see I have a true community of friends in security that are always there helping others step up and step forward in their own unique way. For me personally that has been doing things like recording podcasts, teaching yoga four times a week before work, starting partnerships with inspirational security leaders, running a men's group, and pressing send on this chapter for a book! I'm exceptionally grateful for each of them and will pay that debt forward by showing up to support others.

I wish you well on your own journey and may you find the thread that runs through your life!

When you do I invite you to grab it and follow it, it may just lead you towards your next fulfilling adventure.

See you on a beach somewhere, hacking strategies!

"Let go of who you think you're supposed to be; embrace who you are." Brene Brown

Chapter 2

Name: Chris Windley
Job Title: CEO & Founder
Company: Cyber Security Valley UK
Location: Leicestershire, UK

After monitoring all the sensors, communications, radar, sonar it was clear we were being attacked.

Exocet………. ready, Sea Wolf………. Ready, FIRE!

When I left the Navy, I had reached the object of my ambitions at that time; to fight a ship with electronic means (mainly) and to work with my Captain and the other senior officers. Communications Intelligence (Commint) and Electronic Warfare (EW and ECM – Electronic Counter Measures) being focus areas of mine.

I left to work for Ferranti – manufacturer of many of the computer systems for Navy ships at that time and worked with Defence Ministries around the world building Communications and Weapons Systems simulators for them.

That was a time of rapid change in computing systems which might be best explained by saying that in a very few years computers used at the heart of simulation systems went from massive mainframe computers and peripherals (disc and tape) to Personal Computers and Servers.

In my civilian companies I saw warehouses once crammed full of computers shrink to a lonely box in the middle of the floor. We put them in, and we took them out.

The pace of change in the 80's and 90's was frightening to some but exciting to me. Moore's Law in front of my eyes.

I started predicting what was coming and researching what was coming.

I believed in the statement that "The Network was the Computer". Data Networks connected everything. So, I jumped from computers to networks – I became a "Nethead". (Bellheads were people who had grown up from the telephone systems world). The two worlds were colliding fast.

I helped build superfast multi-protocol fibre optic networks for anyone who would buy them. The people who bought them had huge amounts of data that needed moving in nano seconds; and they had the money to do it. Local, Metropolitan and National networks. Obviously at the time fibre optic cable was being laid at the bottom of the oceans and connecting continents. So, we also could connect organisations in London and New York.

I spotted an opportunity as my investment banking customers sought ever higher speeds and lower latency. Router based networks were being replaced with switch-based networks in local and metro areas. These switches and their operation became my infatuation. I started a company called LanSwitch with 2 colleagues which evolved into Voyager Networks and Internetworking between London and New York and nationally across the UK.

When we started, we worked from our homes in the Midlands, Bristol and Leeds and used the just emerging Internet, laptops and pretty soon cloud based apps together with old style phones and fax machines to grow the business rapidly. We have worked from our homes ever since – nearly 30 years.

We built our own national fibre and copper network; and provided our clients with a Managed Service Network based on that network; always high speed and always state of the art – leading edge but not bleeding edge.

I have built many companies from my home. Working from home and remotely became my passion, living in the country and occasionally going to meetings in our offices or client's offices. We worked from home before working from home became necessary during the Pandemic. Nothing changed for us.

Cyber Security began to emerge as a concern of course but we were focused on merging voice, video and data over high speed networks and creating unified communications solutions, early web conferencing solutions, IP Telephony solutions working with Cisco, 3Com, and other unifying solutions. Cisco, for example, began to show very advanced video conferencing and holographic imaging solutions.

High speed networks were the key to everything as far as I was concerned. If you were rolling out fibre somewhere then that was great to me.

Although an engineer, I was focused on business strategy, sales, and marketing I had Cyber Security in mind as something that I needed to be aware of but not my area of specialisation. Also bear in mind that I am always looking for "the next big wave" after high speed networks and unified communications. Cyber Security is a huge wave of challenge and opportunity.

At this time I am investing in companies in the USA, Israel and the UK, helping rapidly scale them in the same way that we rapidly scaled Voyager Networks and Internet (after building it for 7 years it was sold for $110 Million in 2000 just before the dot com crash). I have also researched and developed systems and solutions to acquire leads and customers rapidly on a global basis working with Pioneers in this area like HubSpot – the Inbound Marketing specialist.

In the Cisco days one of my Navy colleagues, Tim Moran, was working in the same area on IP Telephony and Unified

Communications. Tim was a W.E.O. like me but on Nuclear Subs. At that time, he was also focused on networks.

Tim had started specialising in Cyber Security at Cisco and then gone on to various other companies that were working in cyber security with the same companies (investment banks etc) in which we were building high speed networks.

He was working from home too and he realised that he was a "back door" in cyber security terms, to those investment banks. If someone hacked him at home, then they could potentially get access to those investment banks as well.

Tim set about cyber securing himself; he realised that it was complicated, expensive and time consuming so he created a company to solve these issues and create - to use the LuJam Cyber strapline - *"an Enterprise Level Cyber Security solution, that was simple to use, for the price of a mobile phone contract"*.

A solution aimed at SMB's, Home and Remote workers this caught my attention and we spoke about it a number of times and I tried to give him my best advice.

He started in the SetSquared Incubator in The Engine Shed, Bristol and then won his way into the GCHQ/NCSC/Wayra Cyber Security Incubator.

We discussed "Route to Market "Strategy and I believed that the best route was via partners. I joined LuJam to build that Channel Partner network, something I have done many times before. I have built companies that sold direct (Voyager), and indirect (5i) and Managed Service Providers was our best route to market. Working in the GCHQ/NCSC/Wayra Cyber Accelerator in Cheltenham I was in the centre of Cyber Security, perhaps in the world.

We worked closely with IASME (as of April 2020 the sole Cyber Essentials partner) to create a solution that is broadly a "Continuous Monitoring against the Cyber Essentials standard solution. It started as something else and is being developed beyond Cyber Essentials to Compliance and Risk Scoring but that is another story.

I worked hard to understand the GCHQ/NCSC/IASME/Cyber Essentials strategy and objectives and also to place Cyber Essentials within the global picture of ISO 27001 and NIST.

For a time, I even worked with Canadian representatives on their SMB Cyber Security strategy and have some great connections there.

In the last 9 months I have worked with BRIM (Business Resilience International Management) and the Police on the roll out of the Cyber Resilience Centres. Here my knowledge of the SMB Cyber Security Market, Cyber Essentials, Cyber Essentials Certification Bodies and my ability to acquire partners rapidly has come to the fore as the 10 Cyber Resilience Centres were needed to be rolled out as soon as possible given the dramatically rising number of Pandemic related Cyber-attacks.

These are a fabulous initiative to support UK business in protecting themselves against Cyber-attack.

Working in Cheltenham and Bristol and being half Welsh (Welsh Cyber is booming!) gave me a unique perspective on cyber security activity in the area. There was a desperate need to document and promote the existence of a thriving ecosystem.

There are many exciting and important Cyber Park developments and cyber security success stories and yet these are not known even within the cyber security community of the UK.

With a number of business connections and friends we decided to address this issue and create "Cyber Security Valley UK", an area spanning the Midlands, Wales, and the South West; another way of describing this area is M5/M50/M4 Triangle. This connects and combines the economic regions of the Midlands Engine (West and East Midlands) and the Western Powerhouse (Cheltenham, Salisbury, Swansea triangle).

We work closely with Lisa Ventura at the UK Cyber Security Association and with all existing Cyber Hubs, Centres, Clusters and Organisations.

The reality is that companies seeking a base in the UK or Europe tend to look, for many reasons, to Ireland, Holland and London and we really have to work together in order that we can raise the profile of the ecosystem nationally and globally.

The Pandemic has opened a Pandora's box and broken the dam in terms of working from home and remotely. We believe that Cyber Security Valley is a perfect place from which to work living in very beautiful areas like the Malverns or Cotswolds or Black Mountains and traveling short distances into a local Cyber Hub such as Skylon Park or Golden Valley or Tramshed.

Companies are telling their staff that they will not have to commute into e.g. London and so they are moving to country and coast and selling up in the cities.

Chapter 3

Name: Ciaran Durnin. CISSP
Job Title: Threat & Vulnerability Management Offerings Manager & Fujitsu Distinguished Engineer
Company: Fujitsu
Location: Derry, Northern Ireland

My first experience of computing came around 1989 as a Primary 4 pupil in Derry, Northern Ireland. Outside school there were frequent abhorrent terrorist attacks. Inside, I had discovered an Archimedes. Our school had one and it was in our classroom. Eventually, I did some schoolwork peppered with some gaming at home on an Amstrad CPC464.

Fast forward to 1999 and having completed A-Levels, I was off to university to study Music. In the intervening years, computing and technology was pushed to the darkest corner of my musical brain. I found myself enjoying the student life outside of class rather than in the class. Against the backdrop of the troubles in Northern Ireland, going to study music with the friends I had since primary school was a natural and safe progression.

This academic course was beginning to grate a little. I had no interest in the history of Mozart's Marriage of Figaro, yet somehow, I had managed to be offered a full-time job as a peripatetic music tutor for the local education authority before graduation. Great news, my parents thought, a solid job upon graduation. Luckily, I had incredible foresight to turn it down. I knew it wouldn't be the career for me despite the relative job security and great holidays! Whilst at university, I transferred into a Music Technology major and this rekindled my love of technology. The curiosity was resurfaced. The impact of a few lines of code that could generate sounds on a computer was pretty exciting for me. I started to understand the power of computers albeit in an unconventional setting. So, having graduated with a degree, I knew I was faced with a real problem. Had I just wasted 4 years at university?

Following graduation, I worked in a bank call centre and then a technical support call centre whilst waiting on a placement within Northern Ireland Civil Service. At 22, I resigned myself to being condemned to a life of filing and paperwork. Then, the next stroke of luck came. I was placed into a help desk role as the hiring manager needed someone to answer the phone and reset passwords on an NT4 domain. My previous experience, troubleshooting large format printers over the phone had helped me get a full time, IT job. This was the start. Where would it end?

This entry level job introduced me to corporate IT. In this first role, I was privileged to work for a fantastic manager who supported my desire to 'convert' to a technical role. She agreed to fund my first technical certification, Microsoft Certified Desktop Support Technician. A conversation with Anne, my manager, outlined that whilst she was always supportive of people willing to learn, she rarely funded it if she didn't think the individual would have the dedication to the learning. It was an important milestone for many reasons, not least because I knew it would help deflect the questions related to my degree. I knew I had to prove to any future employers that I have solid technical credentials and that 'tech jobs' weren't a stop gap between gigs.

TIP: Invest in yourself before you expect others to do so. It's your career and you are responsible for your learning.

Having obtained the certification, I thought I had made it. The grandeur of the MCDST moniker allowed me to switch off the curiosity for a few months. Then, I discovered Server and network administration and the curiosity resurfaced. I began to realise that I had outgrown imaging PCs and resetting passwords. I had discovered group policy and the ability to secure a PC with a few centrally managed settings. With great power comes great responsibility and sometimes my curiosity caused some server outages. I also picked up another Microsoft Certified Professional qualification for server administration. I also studied for Cisco CCNA at night. I knew this one would be time well spent as understanding how networks were built and operated would be a core part of any future career moves. This also reinforced some advice I got from my father "knowledge is difficult to obtain but easily carried".

Gradually I had outgrown the role and with opportunities to progress constrained by the promotion competitions within public sector, I took a leap and secured a job with Fujitsu. Peace time in Northern Ireland, however fragile, changed the future for people in my generation and those who followed. Fujitsu decided to open a second Northern Ireland base in Derry. It is probably fair to say that this would not have happened if we still had "Troubles". It's also important to highlight the continuing technical self-investment that made securing this job possible. I still remember the technical screening test showing network diagrams and describing issues. I'm sure that obtaining technical certifications allayed concerns about by musical past. This was 2007 and I was amongst the first cohort through the door.

I spent a few years in various infrastructure related roles and by now I had progressed to technical architecture. There were some common themes amongst these roles. Securing desktop builds with policy, anti-virus, and device encryption, creating firewall rule sets to secure application traffic, and venturing into two factor authentication solutions. This was infinitely more interesting to me than the things I had been doing. I was increasingly curious about this security field. I worked with someone who was CISSP certified and at the time it felt like being in the presence of greatness. It also inspired me for future study. I knew that I wanted to achieve this certification.

Lady Luck once again shone down as around this time (2011), Fujitsu's security business was expanding and thanks to having a good network within Fujitsu and (hopefully) a decent reputation, I decided that this was the path for me. Within a number of weeks, I had transitioned to a security architecture role. Initially, I would say that credibility was a bit of an issue for me. There are different views on solutions and their implementation. I was someone who hasn't grown up "on the tools" and realised that designing solutions which I wouldn't operate long term could cause some tension. To overcome this, it became apparent quite quickly that communication and the use of language is crucially important to building trust and relationships. Engaging the engineers early and involving them helps to quickly build a shared and common understanding.

TIP: Communication skills are vital, involve key stakeholders early and frequently.

Now back to CISSP, this felt like the next logical step for me. I had initially set my sights a lot lower, by aiming for the Security certification. I am not intending to diminish this qualification, but a conversation with an associate from primary school suggested that I had good knowledge already and to aim a little higher. This series of conversations also influenced my behaviours. This guy, whom I hadn't spoken with in 10+ years was happy to share his experience and some of his experiences with the 6-hour behemoth CISSP exam. Thankfully CISSP is now a 4-hour exam – go for it!

TIP: Aim high, you know more than you think.

By now I had built up a lot of experience in Security Incident and Event Management solutions and had become the lead architect in this discipline within Fujitsu. I still find SIEM fascinating. I've seen a major transition from SIEM being a compliance tick box to the focal point for security operations teams and a core part of organisations' defences.

Further inspiration came to me from an unlikely source. Technology vendors spend vast sums of money in their partner ecosystems. At one SIEM vendor event the guest speaker, an Olympic and world championship medalist, reminded the audience that "the past is for reference, not for residence." This became a Eureka moment for me. From this point I would no longer dwell on the musical past.

In 2016, I progressed to managing a team of technical architects within Fujitsu's security business. This initially felt quite daunting as these guys were teammates. Now, I was their manager. This was a huge leap forward for my career. It was also the first time in many years where I felt under significant pressure to prove myself once again.

I knew I had a challenge on my hands here, in terms of learning how to manage people as well as dealing with commercial and financial aspects too. I had a fantastic manager who was willing to take a chance on me as I knew I was probably least experienced candidate. This experience reinforces another valuable lesson in terms of seeking out great managers to work with. This management role also highlighted the need to be comfortable discussing non-technical issues such involving contracts, finances, and people management.

Earlier in my career I encountered a manager who had followed a similar path in terms of going from teammate to manager and candidly it was a horrible experience. I was determined not to be the same as that individual. This ex-colleague wanted people who worked for him, not with him. This is a subtle yet important distinction.
If you do pursue the managerial route, consider this approach.

TIP: Develop soft skills with as much passion as you develop technical skills.

Time and time again in my career, I have tried to follow a 3-4-year cycle. By this, I mean that I want to challenge myself and to move into a new role. In simple terms I view this as learning the role in the first year, building on the role in the second year. In the third year, I then tend to seek out new opportunities which will enable me to further develop. Whilst the timings are certainly not fixed, this approach has served me well since graduation in 2003. When I have been mentoring people in the past, I frequently discuss my views on experience. For me, doing the same role for 20 years is akin to 1 years' experience 20 times. I prefer to look at my career as blocks of different experiences. The cumulative effect will hopefully see me in a position of leadership with a well-rounded experience base across technical, solution, commercial and people management. I urge anyone who is embarking upon a career in Cyber Security to seek out different experiences and opportunities to widen their skills.

It would be remiss of me to ignore some of the challenges I faced. Regardless of how you progress your career, it's vitally important to embrace your weaknesses as well as your strengths. I have had some really difficult moments in my career where I didn't ask for help nor discuss some of the things that were building on my mind. I have always held myself to high standards. Sometimes, you've got to give yourself a break and accept that you need help. Find an ally, if not your manager and don't carry the burden alone. I've had those sleepless nights.

I've also found out a lot about my personality type and would recommend to anyone that the research some of these profiling tools such as Myers Briggs. For me, it explains a lot about how and why I do what I do and enables me to be aware of my blind spots so as not to fall into them too often.

Earlier in the piece, I had an open question as to whether I had wasted 4 years at university. On reflection, I don't believe I did. Aside from some great life experiences, I was lucky to re-ignite the curiosity I had at primary school for computing. I can honestly state that I certainly didn't think 15 years ago I would have established a career in Cyber Security.

My curiosity led to this point in my career and as I write this, I am halfway through an MSc in Applied Cyber Security. This is my way of resolving the university question and challenging myself to continually grow. Next stop, who knows?

TIP: Maintain a growth mindset, embrace your curiosity, and let it take you with it.

Finally, to quote a poem called 'Dream Big', "*Persist. Because with an idea, détermination, and the right tools, you can do great things. Let your instincts, your intellect, and your heart guide you.*"

I wish you every success as you build your career in Cyber Security.

Chapter 4

Name: James Bore
Job Title: Director
Company: Bores Consultancy Ltd
Location: London, UK

I get asked a lot about how to break into the cyber security industry. Frankly, I don't really have an answer. There is no point in my career path I could really point to and say 'there, that's where I was in the cyber security industry, that's how you can break in'. It was a much more natural and gradual progression, and there was no destination in mind at the start. This isn't going to be a step by step walkthrough of how to get into the industry (though it is one I strongly suggest entering), but more of a vague ramble illustrating that there might be other ways than those you hear about most often. My career has been characterised more by generous doses of luck, continuous curiosity, and some great mentors than any meticulously planned career path. I'm not against the meticulously planned career path, and for some people it seems to work, I just want to make sure the alternatives get spoken about for those who don't have everything figured out. I also haven't had many obstacles put in my way over the years – I've benefited from healthy serendipity, a good education (a below-average state school, but academically and technologically-forward parents made up for it), and a lack of much in the way of systemic prejudice against me (the worst I've had to deal with is comments over the fact I keep my hair long, and only one company ever suggested I should cut it if I wanted to work there).

While there are obvious cases of people who have 'broken into' cyber security, I'd make a personal strong recommendation for 'wandering vaguely into' cyber security instead. There are skills and experience you pick up along the way that you will not find going straight into a dedicated cyber role, and they can help you avoid some common mistakes later on.

In 1999 I had everything pretty much figured out, I was going to study physics at university, find some sort of job involving the degree and live happily ever after.

In 2001 I quit my degree course, bored of the teaching, and not feeling like I was learning anything, separated from my wife at the time for personal reasons, and fell apart for a while.

I had gone into university determined not to do something centring around computers, as that had been what everyone expected me to do. I'd had a computer and internet access before the local schools and had been crawling around under desks of my parent's home office plugging in BNC connectors and troubleshooting their network for years. I had, more than anyone else I knew, grown up with computers and was determined not to get typecast into what everyone expected.

Personal advice here – rebelling against expectations for the sake of doing so is sometimes not worthwhile.

Since I now wasn't doing much other than working part time as a school IT technician, I was gently encouraged to try out a few different courses. The first was one of those boot camps, guaranteeing you a job things. I did get a job out of it – driving about

200 miles a day to fix people's computers for them at only slightly more than the cost of petrol at the time. That was career path attempt one, and when it failed a year later[1] I went back to living with my parents and trying again.

The second attempt was more successful, I went to a boot camp, got my first professional certification, and found that either the intensive learning model or the material, or something about it (possibly the great food as it was a residential training provider), just worked for me. Part-way through the boot camp I booked my Security+ exam along with the MCSE exam they were providing, because it maximised the number of qualifications I'd be ending up with.

I cannot recommend schools enough as a way to learn technology and security. In these days of managed services, it doesn't apply to quite the same level, but at that point everything was done in-house, on a shoestring or no budget, and we were just entering the early days of data protection being a concern. I, and later a part time assistant, had responsibility for 500 classroom computers, with a pool of 2000 eager amateur pen testers let loose on them six hours a

---

[1] The company had been steadily losing staff, so I was now being asked to cover a wider and wider area – the final straw was when I was told that they were capping mileage payments at £15, regardless of how long the trip took or how far it was, and then asked me to take a job in Scotland – 300 miles away.

day, and highly motivated to bypass any filters which were put in place to limit internet access or prevent games.

You'll also end up with a pool of users who aren't big fans of using the technology in any sensible way, have access to vast amounts of sensitive data, and a limited understanding of security. If you're working in a school, view this as an opportunity to practise your security advocacy skills rather than a frustration.

Of course, schools can also be a stressful environment, and I did have some very unpleasant encounters with staff members who looked down on anyone who wasn't teaching with a degree of contempt. It was far from universal, but it definitely happened, and sadly no longer being a student at a school does not mean bullying ends. I am told things are better today, but it would be safe to say a lot of my conflict resolution skills, as well as my developed willingness to give absolutely no slack whatsoever to bullies, came out of this period.

That background made me learn that there is no such thing as perfect, and it is always better to be moving than standing still and waiting for the ideal solution. You can always change direction later if a better solution becomes available, but unless you have a TARDIS[2] you can't go back in time and start earlier on. Security

---

[2] I did promise I'd get some Doctor Who jokes in, given the obvious opportunity from the title. See if you can spot the others.

threats move fast, and it's better to be doing something against them now while trying to consider the best way than waiting until you have the perfect plan in place.

After working through several schools, I moved to tech support for a company providing management systems to schools. Again, there's that concern over data, only now I was encountering it from the other side – discovering how the permissions I'd struggled to get teachers to accept in schools were carefully considered and planned. This was also where I was incredibly lucky and came across the first of my mentors.

I was interested in technology, read a lot, and spent a lot of time learning. I read up and experimented with the technologies the products were based on, as well as more generally, and began to apply that knowledge. I also spent a lot of time talking with the new architect who had come in for a virtualisation project, mainly expressing a genuine interest in the work he was doing. A few months later I was working for him rather than on the support desk, helping to build something that's now commonplace, but at the time was still somewhat revolutionary – a cloud SaaS solution.
Again, being interested in the subject, spending a lot of time reading and researching around it, and a lot of time playing with the technologies in my own time helped me grow into the role. I spent

two and a half years with that company, which would turn out to be the longest time I would spend at a company. The architect there would also turn out to be the first of the people I now consider mentors, and I picked up from him an approach to leadership and technology that I still follow to this day.

A quick aside, you'll occasionally hear people say that you must stay with a company for three years, or even two years, or sometimes even one year, or it will be harder to get new roles. They aren't completely wrong, but it is all about your view and how you present yourself. Over the last twenty years I have had nineteen different roles (more if I count the last year, but that one's a bit exceptional so let's ignore it). The shortest of those roles was two months. A couple of those roles I didn't leave on great terms (though to be clear it was me leaving them), but with the vast majority it was a pleasant experience for all.

I would occasionally get asked if I was a contractor in interviews or why I have short term roles. My answer was generally along the lines of the following, and if you're like me then feel free to modify/steal the answer as appropriate: "I've always been in permanent roles, and have found that companies often bring me in to resolve a specific problem or complete a specific project. When that's finished I, and they, usually find that I'm doing day to day management, which is not a role I'm particularly suited for as I like to build. As you'll see, where I've been able to find new challenges within a role, I've happily stayed on, and where I haven't I've made sure that anything I've built is effectively handed over within the company and parted on good terms to find new challenges. In fact, that's why I'm leaving my current role, and they are aware that I'm looking."

That movement between different roles whenever they weren't challenging was rewarding, both financially and in terms of experience. I had new challenges, and had to quickly adapt to new cultures, industries, technologies, and ways of doing things. There are people who say that you can learn a new language well enough to use in six months of full immersion within it, and the same applies to companies. There is nothing wrong with committing to, and staying with, a company for multiple years, but don't let people tell you that it is the only way to build a career. There are other options, and what works for one person won't work for others.

Your other option for that sort of career path is to be a contractor, of course, but there are issues you should be aware of – particularly if you're in the UK with IR35. Even if you're doing short stints with an employer, it's often worth being an employee for the benefits, such as sick leave, paid holiday, and development, unless you've already developed the experience that your income as a contractor can cover any gaps. There's a degree of security, and opportunity to experiment more safely, as an employee for a good company that you don't get when you are self-employed in some form.

After that longer-than-planned aside, back to the main thread of the story. We come to 2015 – I had a job I very much enjoyed, had overcome my nerves about public speaking through getting involved with a movement called Café Scientifique[3], and was just coasting along thinking about what I should do next.

In 2016 I was forced to take some time out to think about things. I came down with viral arthritis a few days after making our wedding rings with my now-wife. That meant essentially, I woke up one morning, moved to get out of bed, screamed, and collapsed sobbing on the ground. After being pretty much carried down the stairs and to the hospital I was told I had gout. About a month later, when it has just continued getting worse and spread from my ankles to every join in my body, a specialist I'd been referred to suggested it might

---

[3] Overcoming my nerves did not mean I didn't, or don't, feel them. I'm just as scared of public speaking as anyone else I know, maybe a little less as I've had practice and made every mistake possible by now, and seen the consequences aren't that bad. I highly recommend it to anyone interested in getting involved in security, as not only does it bring exposure but really helps with communication and presentation skills which are absolutely vital.

be auto-immune arthritis triggered by a virus, and put me on steroids and really good painkillers.

About two weeks later I was able to move around again and felt fine. Side effects of the steroids were boundless energy, and sleeping 3-4 hours a night at most, so I had time, was no longer as distracted by pain, and bored out of my mind. Initially I tried going back to work but was told that they didn't want me in until I was off the steroids (understandable, but more than a little frustrating) so I had to find things to do instead.

I really did want to go back to work, and my employer at the time would not have me in while I was on the medication, so I started a bit of job hunting. I also started reading around, studying, just doing anything I could to keep myself busy. And I applied for a part-time Master's. Having quit university the first time, and a long time earlier, I didn't have a degree or even any viable credits, but they were willing to take my industry experience into account and accept me to the course.

In September, shortly after coming off the medication (coming off steroids is not a short process, and if I had any recurrence it's likely I would still be on them today as they tend not to take chances), and getting over some minor issues coming off the painkillers, I started a new role alongside my part time course.

As well as being a fantastic team, this role gave me the option of being almost fully remote and flexible, and earned my loyalty in return (during WannaCry I was on my honeymoon in Japan and had the joy of being woken up at 4am – we still sorted the issue and avoided any instances). Turns out that having plenty to do, having the flexibility and autonomy to use my time as best I saw fit rather than sitting at a desk 8 hours a day and travelling 2 hours a day either side, made a huge difference. During the same year I was working through my Master's, I was also very much enjoying work, starting to speak regularly at conferences, going to various roundtable events, and training for a Spartan trifecta. And yet despite all that I had more free time than ever before.

This would also be where I encountered the second person I'd consider a mentor, a long term senior manager in the company who knew everyone, and everything about the structure and showed me how to work with or around the system to make things happen. I don't want to suggest it was a case of bypassing controls or procedures, but she showed me how important it was to consider people in building a system – the best system in the world is useless if no one uses it, and worse than useless if you have to force people to use it.

I left that company after two years, having done everything I could for them and not having anywhere else to go internally. After that, until recently, things are fairly unremarkable except for one experience which taught me lessons I think are very important and need to be shared.

I worked for a few months for a start-up that I could best describe as toxic. That's the most polite description I can manage. I was brought on to take charge of their cyber security, entirely, and supposedly reporting to the board. The lesson that I want people to learn from this is that sometimes you just need to recognise the environment is poisonous, the company is doomed, and you should get the hell out of there as fast as you possibly can.

The first clue was that it was a start-up which was completely against any remote or flexible working, expecting a minimum of nine-hour days, and unwilling to put any budget into security. The CEO was theoretically the ultimate authority on everything, and happily overruled the board who never had an opportunity to object but turned out to be little more than a mouthpiece for the main shareholder's advisor.

There was no understanding of the technology, which is worrying in a financial technology company, no concern about security or fraud protection, and I left after being told to get them PCI DSS compliance. That is, I was told to get PCI DSS compliance, not to make them compliant with PCI DSS.

My response may not have been the most diplomatic, in sending a message to the board that I believed they were risking the company and customers by ignoring security needs, and proposing a plan to address those needs for (what I thought) a very reasonable budget, with a very reasonable timeline.

Toxic companies exist, toxic work environments exist, and you may hit a time when your personal code of ethics conflicts at a fundamental level with what a company is trying to do. At that point I can only recommend leaving as fast as you can. I ended up having a near breakdown over just a few months and handing my notice in without anywhere else to go as I simply had to get out. Your integrity, your own personal ethics, are simply not a price worth paying.

The company is still around, but from what I gather it won't be much longer before it's exterminated[4]. I won't go into too much detail about specifics for obvious reasons, nor name the company, this is just a lesson I would like to spare anyone else having to learn

---

[4] Another of those Doctor Who jokes I promised.

through painful experience. If you feel something is very, very wrong, it's worth listening. Equally importantly, if you feel that things are wrong reach out to your network and the community, people will help and support more than you'd believe possible, and many will have encountered similar experiences or know someone who has.

We're now nearly up to date, and a fairly dramatic shift in my career path along with very rapid learning. My most recent role as an employee started in a slightly atypical manner – in the interview, talking through past short roles, I was asked if there was a reason I'd never gone down the contracting or independent route. All I could say was that I'd only ever had experience as an employee and had never really had an opportunity to transition.

I've mentioned that toxic companies and employers exist, but it's important to know that good companies and employers are out there too, and one that sees the potential in employees and is willing to look beyond classical employment models is worth its weight in gold. My last employer was very much one of these, offering me a fixed term contract to give me an opportunity to work with them over several months as a semi-external consultant with a wide remit, and transitioning at the end into a different business relationship.

I'm not going to say that type of employer is common, but if you find one then treasure them and grab the opportunity with both hands and feet.

While I call them my last employer, it isn't quite true. In September 2020 I moved to employment in my own consultancy, meaning that my new employer is me (there are lots of jokes I can, and sometimes do, make about being an arsehole boss who pays under minimum and makes me work long hours), although since I'm employed by a company that I own it's not technically self-employment. It's definitely a path that's open as your career in security develops. If you do go down that route, I strongly recommend getting yourself a good accountant.

Going your own way is, frankly, terrifying in parts as I have no idea if I'll have enough work to bring money in, and there's a lot of trying out different ideas and having to learn different skills (including trying to become a salesman) in a very short space of time.

On the other hand, if you're running out of challenges in a corporate environment, it's definitely an approach worth looking into as an alternative to climbing the ladder.

Chapter 5

Name: Mark Shawa - www.markshawa.com
Job Title: Conscious Inspirational Leader, Cyber Security Awareness Evangelist
Company: Vodacom South Africa
Location: South Africa/Zambia/Digitally Everywhere

Part 1: Why and who is Mark?
"Inspired to Inspire" (Shawa, 2020).

I believe that we are stronger and better when we are woven in trust and authenticity. My journey to cyber is not an ordinary one, it has come with its up and downs that have led me to where I am today. It has brought me to self-discovery as a teacher, as a thinker, and a storyteller. Taking advantage of all opportunities at my disposal, I have now become an inspiration to many others because of my openness to learning new things and sharing my expertise. The "WHY?" is simple, it is to create safe spaces for all, so that we can feel inspired to be our authentic selves and in turn, inspire others to do the same. Now that I've shared the "why" I do the things I do, and "who I am", let's get into the story of how I got into cyber security.

Part 2: The Beginning.

I've always been curious. From as far back as I can remember, I have always wanted to know how things work. I have always wanted to know why things are and the meaning behind the existence of the world we live in. One memorable moment that I have the privilege of looking at even now is an image of a two-year-old me, smiling with a landline telephone on my hand.

My mother believed that my love for the telephone was influenced by my constructive speech at a noticeably young age, however what she did not realize was that I was mimicking what I saw. My parents spent time on the phone talking to friends and family, and I wanted that too.

My engagement with computers started at the age of five or six. For those who don't know, I'm from Zambia and(there) having a computer at the age of five is not necessarily common, especially in the 90s. My father though, a seasoned engineer had the privilege of owning one, an old school PC desktop from which I started exploring the tech space. When I started interacting with the computer my parents made sure that whatever I was doing with it, was educational. At the time, there was a program called Encarta that was still on a CD-ROM. Encarta was full of fun mazes, quizzes on general knowledge and other "smart" features which further inflicted my curiosity as a child to dig deeper into the meaning of things. I believe it was at that moment that I began to think differently from what a normal five-year-old would think. With my newfound knowledge from Encarta, I felt invincible.

I began my academia journey and really sprinted forward. I started practicing for my grade 7 examinations in the year 2000. I was still in grade 4, crazy right?

Unfortunately, my dream to write my grade 7 examination in grade 6 did not happen. Due to family complications, in December 2001 I found out that I had to complete my primary school in Zimbabwe. I was devastated to say the least, my plans as a ten-year-old were taken from me without my approval. Thus, began my nomadic life which would shape my values and experiences that I had known from a Zambian perspective to a global one.

Part 3: Eat or Be Eaten.

The rollercoaster ride began in 2002, however without boring you with all details, let me give you a brief history of my schooling journey between 2002 and 2009. I did grade 6 to 7 at Rhodes Estate Preparatory School, Form 1 to 4 at Plumtree High School and finally completed my A-Levels at Hillcrest Technical School back in Zambia. All these were boarding schools, and equally far away from home. The horror of not being able to contact my family at the age of 11 gave me terrible anxiety. Oh, did I mention I had to learn and write examinations in Ndebele during my school time in Zimbabwe? Talk about adding salt to a wound. So, what do you get when you mix an 11-year-old, foreign national far away from home, scared and doesn't understand the language to be able to communicate with his peers? You get an innovator.

I began to think of ways that I could contact my family, pass my Ndebele essays and still fit in with the people. This is probably where I started my journey in social engineering. I learnt how to gain the trust of my peers which would allow me to get them to help me with what I needed; you can call this "hacking" the human.

One standout moment for me is when I needed a phone to contact my family. Cell phones were not allowed in the school premises, but my senior had one. I had gathered that it was possible to hack a landline by using certain frequencies that would match the tone associated with the number being dialled. In short, I could make free calls from the school landline because each number had a unique frequency, and I wouldn't have to physically touch the phone. All I needed was my senior's cell phone. He had a Nokia 3310 with monophonic tones which you would hear whenever you dial numbers, so I thought to myself what if it has the same frequency as the landline phone? So, I tested it out and voila! I managed to call home. I was scared and thrilled at the same time. It was exhilarating to say the least. I made phone calls to home, friends and all I needed to do, was simply give some of my food to my senior so that I had access to his cell phone.

This went on through primary and even in high school. Unfortunately, in achieving these hacks of people and technology, my ethics began to fade. I had to lie and manipulate to achieve the hacks and because of the thrill I got from it, I justified it by waying it was harmless, so I thought. I was wrong! One day, my

father asked me about our phone bill, and
I rightly denied any involvement with it. He called everyone who was receiving calls from our landline and they all had one person in common, Me! He immediately cut our phone line and that was the end of my phone hacks. He also took the internet away from everyone because of me. If you remember the 2000s well enough, dial-up connection was the only way to access the internet, so what do you get when you mix a teenager, with no internet and phone access? An even bigger social engineer!

Part 4: The South African Jungle, Survival of the Fittest.

Fast forward to November 2009, I was awaiting my A-level results whilst frantically deciding which university to go to. I knew what I wanted to do, I wanted to do Law. I wanted to be a bad ass advocate who would win cases. Raised by the hit series *"Law and Order,"* with multiple debate awards and a sharp brain to make a case out of anything, I strongly felt I would be a law practitioner. I am sure you have heard the saying *"All Lawyers are Liars,"* that is exactly what my dad said when I told him I want to be one. I objected frantically, but truth be told, I had told lies to get what I wanted so he wasn't far from the mark. He told me do something with technology since I enjoyed being behind the computer for hours. I searched for the best computer degrees and found Computer Science and Information

Systems. I had no real clue of what it was. I told my dad I want to do it and received the nod of approval. My family is big on science, so I understand why my dad was excited in my change of choice. I applied to the University of KwaZulu-Natal in Pietermaritzburg, South Africa. I was accepted and took another turn in my nomadic academic life.

In February 2010, I began my tertiary education. This is what most parents look forward to, sending their child to university so they can get a good education which would eventually kick start their career. Remember, I mentioned that I had no clue of what Computer Science and Information Systems was about? It gets worse. My degree was defined to include Mathematics and Statistics as majors alongside Computer Science and I picked Physics as an elective module. I knew I was playing with fire, but I was a bit too arrogant to admit it.

My first semester in University was great, apart from the part that required me to focus on programming. Computer Science was not really the science of computing, but more of the application of computing languages to solve problems. In simple terms, I had to know how to solve mathematical problems such as The Fibonacci Sequence, in Java. That is the same as speaking Swahili to a German man about making food. It's possible, but difficult if you do not understand the semantics of the language. In this case, I had the logic to solve the problems but translating it to code and running it was hell. I did not use the fancy IDE's which would auto-populate a method or library you wish to call as you type, I used JGrasp and Notepad to code. My lecturer said if you can code in JGrasp and Notepad then you can code with any of the newer IDE's which he deemed were for dummies. I was the dummy - I needed that auto-populate functionality to guide me with the right syntax. So, I did what I knew best, hack a person to get what I needed to survive the module. One of my friends was a wiz at programming. He did it in high school, so it was like drinking water for him. But every Achilles has a heel. He had three heels, Mathematics, Physics and Statistics. I convinced him to do my coding and add some "errors" and I would help him with the other modules. This worked like a charm until he did not pass his Physics and Mathematics exam. This resulted in him not doing the following modules in semester two. I needed new leverage to ensure that I keep up with passing Computer Science.

Second semester came and I dropped Physics for Psychology. If you haven't picked it up yet, I have way of hacking people and I believed that if I understand some psychological principles, I will be able to understand how to hack people even better. This was not the case, because that semester Psychology 102 was based on Mental Illnesses and my brain lit up like a Christmas tree. I loved the module and began to question why people are the way they are. The childlike curiosity I knew of was set alight. I researched how to merge Computer Science with Psychology and found out that Computer Science and Psychology can co-exist. I was excited but my excitement was to be short lived. For me to continue with Computer Science and Psychology as majors, I had to change my degree from a Bachelor of Science in Computer Science and Information Technology, to a Bachelor of Social Science in Psychology with Computer Science as a second major. Knowing my dad, he was not going to allow me to make that switch. I quickly abandoned the thought of changing degrees. I began to struggle in Computer Science, since I had no one to "hack." I, thus, failed my second semester module. This moment brought me to the realisation that I could not simply get through university with just being smart, I had to work hard too. This was a tough lesson to learn because it meant that I couldn't proceed to my 2nd year Computer Science without successfully passing the previous module. I lost out on one year and my parents were furious with me.

The following years I worked hard until I completed my 1st degree in Computer Science and Information Systems. This was a great feeling - know that I had bagged my first degree. My parents convinced me to do my Honours degree to bolster my chances of getting a job in South Africa. As you know, if you have ever worked in a foreign country with a permit, it is not easy. I had to work ten times harder to just be seen. Not so difficult, because I was determined to be seen.

I changed faculties and moved to the Commerce side of life. The reason for the change was because I wanted to understand Information Systems and Technology from a commercial perspective. I also hated development, so I said my goodbyes to the Computer Science program, but I kept the skills. Honours was a great time because it did not need me to regurgitate information like in my Under Grad. Now I was able to apply the knowledge I was learning to real world problems. My two favourite modules were Managing Information Systems and Information Security. These two modules opened my mind, about how information Systems work and how information can be secured. This allowed me to be innovative with my thinking. I have always been an out of the box thinker because I ask the question "why" a lot, but now I started to think as if there was no box at all. This thinking was inspired by one assignment I had.

My Information Security professor asked the class to read Kevin Mitnick's Books, *The Art of Deception and The Art of Intrusion*. We were required to write book reviews on both. I fell in love with how Mitnick hacked the societal system to get access to basic things like calls and transportation. I resonated with his curiosity. He learnt how to rig the system so that he could get things done. None of it was malicious, but also none of it was legal. I was fascinated, nonetheless. Mitnick made me aware of social engineering and how technology will always do what you ask it to do, but the true hack comes with hacking people. My ability to construct an argument, give it a logical flow, add a fact or two and sound trusting meant that I was a social engineer before it was confirmed by the book. I sooner realised that the best way to make a system better is by understanding how to break it first. I focused my attention on empowering people with knowledge by raising their awareness of what is out there on the big bad web. This brought some form of fulfilment in my life.

My Honours year is still one of my best years to date. I passed with distinctions and got an opportunity to be part of the best graduate program in the country with Vodacom. I had two interviews, one to be a Radio Access Network Graduate and the other was to be a Change and Security Management Graduate in the Networks division. I took the latter because I loved change and security. I was excited and who wouldn't be. I was on the path to my Cyber Security role, so I thought AGAIN.

Part 5: Work-Perception Vs Reality

I want to start with a disclaimer here: what they teach you at school, does not always translate directly into what you will be doing at work. A simple analogy I can use is, you can read how to ride a bike and be an expert in the knowledge of bike riding, but the day you get on that bike, you will fall a lot of times. This was my experience.

In March 2016, I moved to Cape Town to start the graduate program in the Change and Security Department. I would like to know, why do big companies have so many acronyms? I asked my executive if there was a dictionary for all these acronyms because I was not able to keep up, he chuckled. There was no dictionary, this was common Network language. I found myself in a space where I was expected to know what all those terms meant. I felt small, at the time, I was 25 and always in a room full of seasoned experts who had specialised in networks for over 10 years. There was a mountain ahead of me and climbing it was not going to be easy. This did not deter me in any way. I made it a point that I asked as much as I could so that I could learn exponentially. One thing did bother me, that this was not cyber security, and this was just an aspect of it but on governance level and technical level. I was craving for the strategic level, but I couldn't make those calls because I lacked work experience.

I began with understanding how mobile networks work in the telecommunications space. This was not a walk in the park. I never come across mobile networks in university and I felt the weight of the job hitting me. This is when my thinking cap lit up and Instead of trying to absorb all the information, I just asked what the pain points were so that I could solve the problems with the necessary information. My brain is my superpower, so instead of trying to fill it up with information for the sake of it, I would give it what it needs in order to solve a problem uniquely and this is how I navigated from User Management to Logging and Monitoring. I used my skills to gather data and transform it into information with meaning. Logging and Monitoring of users' activity on the network whilst correlating them to valid change requests helped me in the reduction of incident investigation time, in ensuring that users are performing the right work at the right time and most importantly, reducing the number of compliance and security violations. The journey wasn't easy. Most people still took security as a blocker to their work and it meant I had to find ways to advocate for good security behaviour in the workplace. I sooner realised that an expert in Security is usually a horrible communicator.

Luckily, I was able to hone my communication skills and this allowed me to have conversations with other departments about helping them understand why my department did what it did. I believed in giving people unique solutions instead of just telling them what to do. Collaborations were formed in this way and I was proud of the strides I pulled. I was now seen as the go to person to talk to about security related matters within the network division. It wasn't because I was a guru, it was simply because I chose to listen before prescribing a solution.

I spent four years in the Change and Security Department within Networks and had moved from a graduate to a Specialist. I told myself that after five years, I would pursue another opportunity because of my lack of drive in the department I was in. I wanted to implement impactful campaigns that would help shift the perspective of my colleagues in the division but unfortunately it was extremely difficult, especially without leadership support. My flame began to burn out and work began to feel like a chore. I was applying in different areas whilst still improving my area. I was ready to give up security and do anything else just so that I could feel that spark again.

I believe in this saying "If you do not ask, the answer will always be no," so I spoke to my manager about visiting our head office in Midrand so that I could engage with the Technology Security Team. I recall him saying that the budget is tight, and it may not be possible, but he promised to speak to my executive head of department. The answer came back, it was a yes. I worked on myself and grounded myself on the first impression mission. I told myself I needed to show up and make a good impression.

Little did I know that I had already made an impression because news travel fast when you are doing something impactful. I received a message from the Managing Executive of Cyber and he wanted to meet and talk with me about Cyber Security. I told him that we can have coffee together when I am at the head office. He agreed and we had our coffee. That coffee was beautiful because he didn't ask me about what I am good at, he wanted to talk about me and why I love Security. I told him I love it because it never ends, it's a space where innovation is always needed and the best way to keep the juices flowing is by bringing in people of different perspectives. He shared his plan with me and requested that I join his team to lead Cyber Security Awareness and Culture. I was all sorted of shocked! I said yes already but tried to keep calm because, you know, professionalism. The spark came back. I was presented an opportunity to engage with people in a meaningful way and I was given the strategic reigns to do it.

Part 6: Old Flame, New Perspectives

In July 2020, mid pandemic, I started my new role in the Cyber Security Governance, Risk and Compliance department. One thing I can say about starting a new role in a pandemic and from home is that it is not easy, I do not recommend it at all. I appreciate my team and leadership because they availed themselves for me to understand the role better. It is a fast-paced role that requires communication, Public Relations, and marketing skills. How else do you influence people to shift their minds on how to work when they've been working a certain way for 20 odd years? You engage with them!

My role entails of a lot now. I draft communications to the workforce of over 10 000 people regarding Cyber Security. The twist is that I cannot be technical, because 90% of the workforce does not care about that. They care about their work, so I have learnt not to just send out awareness communications, but to communicate in a way that helps people resonate with the message. It is not easy at all, but it is worth it. 10 000 people means 10 000 perspectives but being able to capture even one percent of that means that I have 1 000 people who can help me drive more awareness. Like a snowball, in this new role I've learnt that I don't need to get everyone's attention, I must pay attention to the ones who are already on the same page as me and empower them to empower others in their space. The early adopters of the cyber conscious culture are ambassadors that can get the 70% to shift their perspectives until we get some form of unity. This comes with patience, time, trial as well as error and a lot of push back. I love the role I play because it deals with people.

The recurring theme of my journey into cyber security is people. I started off hacking them for my personal gain, but now, it is for their benefit. I would not call it a hack, but a natural gift to be able to make people feel heard, seen and understood, I'd call it a natural gift so that I can serve them better. Training and Awareness campaigns are not easy at all, and that is why I love them. I get to be creative, relate it to the culture of the organisation and use multiple mediums to get the message across. You do not have to be a Cyber Expert to contribute to the Cyber cause. Your small secure behaviour contributes to the bigger picture which, in totality, is impactful.

Part 7: Closing reMARKs

We are reaching the end of my story in this amazing book, and I would love to leave you with a few things to take away from it. I have learnt a lot in the few months I have been in the actual Cyber Security Space and still am. I don't have the usual qualifications that are expected from someone in my field. I am not certified but definitely going that route when my brain believes it's worth the jump. However if there is something no one can say I don't have, its experience. Experience through personal growth and experience through conversations with seasoned experts. I may only have five years of work experience but I do have over 30 years of conversational experience which I use in my job every day. Most of these experiences you won't learn in a book or classroom, you will learn from engaging with people intentionally.

I have a vision for Cyber Security, and Africa specifically. It is to build an association where we create Cyber Security Conscious Campaigns that are embedded in the culture of Africans to better equip them in the never-ending cyber battle. I believe that the more we can share the quicker we can prepare for what is coming at us, but we will have to work together.

Before I kill you with anecdotes, here are a few takeaways from me to you, and I don't mean fast food:

1. **If you don't ask, the answer will always be no**
   Never be afraid to ask a question. It is okay to admit you do not know. Someone listening with the intention to help you grow understands what it is like to be in the building block phase of your career. So, ASK QUESTIONS.

2. **Be as curious as a kid and allow yourself to make mistakes**

   Now this is a tough one but it's true. Making mistakes is not something you want to be known for but if you don't make a few mistakes, when will you learn? There is always a teaching moment, and it usually comes in the space of making a mistake.

3. **Be open to learning**

   Cyber Security is not linear. There are many paths you can take within the field so learn, learn and learn more. Engage with people, connect with experts, and connect with likeminded Cyber People. This will broaden your knowledge and guide you towards the path of Cyber you love or even the path to get out of it.

Chapter 6

Name: Nathan Chung

Job Title: Senior Cloud Security Consultant

Company: EY

Location: Denver, USA

Introduction

My family originally immigrated to Hawai'i from China in the year 1900, among the tens of thousands of Chinese that came to work on the sugar plantations. I grew up a sci-fi nerd watching TV shows and movies such as: Star Trek, Star Wars, Babylon 5, Battlestar Galactica, and StarGate SG-1. I also really enjoy playing computer games and over the years I played some of the best games of all time including: Sim City, Doom, Prince of Persia, Stellar 7, Spy Hunter, Zaxxon, the Secret of Monkey Island, Diablo, Rebel Assault, Wing Commander, TIE Fighter, Star Control II, Master of Orion 2, Half-Life, X-COM, Civilization I and II, Red Baron, StarCraft, Cities

Skylines, Quake, Halo, Warcraft III, Mass Effect 2, Skyrim, and Fallout 4.

My career was never perfect or consistent and I struggled with depression and career direction. Later in life, I did some soul searching and discovered that I have a mental disability. Being neurodiverse makes me a difficult person to get along with socially. Despite the limitations from being neurodiverse, I did not let that hold me back.

I believe in helping others and making a difference in the world. I was invited to be a judge for the inaugural Cyber Security Woman of the Year Awards in 2019 and won an award for Male Ally of the Year in 2020 for my support of women in IT and cyber security globally.

I also serve on multiple boards including WiCyS Colorado, IGNITE Worldwide, and Spark Mindset. I volunteer at many other organizations as well when time allows. It is a path not frequently travelled, but I find it necessary to make the world a better place and give back to the community.

My first job was working as a clerk at a CPA firm. After I graduated from the University of Hawai'i, I eventually got my first full-time IT job working as an IT technician for the Honolulu Police Department in Honolulu, Hawai'i.

Over the past 20+ years I have been a head of IT, a systems administrator, a help desk specialist, a network administrator, a cyber security auditor, an incident responder, a cyber security architect, and most recently a cyber security consultant specializing in cloud security. I have worked at amazing places such as the Governor's Office in the State of Hawai'i, the Supreme Court of the United States, the United States Postal Service Office of Inspector General, Lockheed Martin, KLA-Tencor, Gymboree, Ross Stores, Sephora, a few start-ups, and most recently EY. It has been a long journey with many ups and downs.

Baptism by Fire

In one of my first IT jobs, the organization was hit by the Nimda worm that crippled IT infrastructure. The manager was away on vacation and the on-call manager was incapable of dealing with the crisis. So, I stepped up, even though I was not a manager and was very much a rookie. After identifying the Nimda worm from system logs and behaviour, I copied the patch and virus cleaning utility to multiple CDs and created instructions.

I then organized groups to go to every facility within the organization to install the patch, clean the virus, and restart systems. By the next day, the virus was cleaned, and all systems were operational. It was my baptism by fire into incident response and all this was done while I was a rookie with the least amount of experience on the entire team and the youngest.

No Budget, No Problem

In another job, I became Head of IT, and took over from a person who had abruptly quit. I inherited a state-wide IT infrastructure that was a mess; it was my first position overseeing such a large scope. Yet I was ready to roll up my sleeves and dive in.

For starters, the organization had only a single server at the core, so it was over-utilized and running out of disk storage space without RAID to provide data storage redundancy. The challenge was how best to upgrade server capacity when the IT budget was cut by almost 80%? I found out that other departments within the organization were throwing out old servers. So, I was able to obtain two newer faster servers that had double CPU capacity, quadruple RAM, and quadruple disk storage space in RAID5 configuration, all at no cost.

Next, the organizations used ancient Compaq PCs running on Celeron CPUs with speed measured in MHz and barely 64MB of RAM. Through a similar process as the servers, I found other departments that had larger IT budgets and were dumping their old Pentium III PCs, so I made phone calls and picked them up. Those PCs had triple CPU power measured in GHz and 2GB of RAM. Within one year, I had upgraded half the organization's PCs, at no cost.

First Cyber Security Job

When I started my first job in cyber security, I was very happy. To transition from IT into cyber security was a great accomplishment of my career.

But then two months later, the manager quit, auditors were on their way to assess PCI-DSS controls, and the IT infrastructure was a mess. The organization was once one of the best places to work in America according to Forbes. However, due to excessive debt, brain drain, and under investment in IT infrastructure, the organization was in trouble.

First, when I asked for advice I was told by older and more experienced cyber security professionals that staying at a firm with so many problems was foolish and stupid, a job that they themselves would not do. Second, it turned out the organization was significantly underpaying me, far below the market rate. Third, with the manager gone, I was thrust into the role of running a failing cyber security program for an entire organization all by myself without any previous experience. No pressure, right?

So, what did I do?

First, I got organized and took a deep dive into the PCI-DSS framework with its 12 high level requirements and audit controls to protect credit card data. Next, I evaluated the current state of IT infrastructure in the organization; it was not pretty. The servers had not been patched in years. The manager had altered vulnerability scan reports to make them appear clean and to give the appearance that patching was not necessary. He had also said patching was not needed because the organization had firewalls. The IT infrastructure itself was ancient and included: flat databases, Windows XP computers, and all running in a single Active Directory domain forest without any segmentation between production, development, and test environments. Any and all of that meant guaranteed non-compliance with PCI-DSS and fines.

Second, I organized, prioritized, and created a road map to bring the entire organization into PCI-DSS compliance. It took about a month to inventory servers, run vulnerability scans, and to patch them all. I got cooperation by being in the trenches with the system administrators and winning executive management support. It took another month to segment the network, setup compensating controls, and to create new documentation.

Third, the auditors saw my predicament and went out of their way to help me. In the cyber security industry, auditors have the reputation of being the villains, but I will never forget them for being there and giving me a helping hand whereas others would have just written a failed audit report. At the end of many long months and long nights, the organization passed with a PCI-DSS report of compliance that satisfied the banks. It was hands down the greatest accomplishment of my cyber security career. I did all that in my first cyber security job, without the title of manager, director, VP, or CISO.

Racism

In another cyber security job, I was the only Asian on the team. I was subjected to racism and discrimination frequently. Not just me, but other teams as well, all because of our race.

On one occasion, the VP was getting frustrated because his email account would get locked out every hour. The team went to work analysing security logs to find the root cause. Because of my previous IT experience, I concluded in less than one hour that the VP's phone was locking out his account due to an old password, but I was ignored. The other guy who had worked for the NSA came to the same conclusion after looking at the logs for a half day; he was celebrated as a hero.

On another occasion, I asked one guy from the team for help with a service ticket. He kept ignoring me. After a few days of asking him for help and being ignored, I asked again. He then responded angrily by yelling a racial slur. I was in shock for days because I had never experienced racism before in the workplace and I did not know how to respond. Then I finally reported the incident to my manager, who was shocked, and HR got involved. When experiencing racism, we should all be willing to stand up for ourselves. We should never tolerate racism.

Moving

I was born and raised in Hawaii. From there I moved to the Washington DC metro area, then to the San Francisco bay area, and on then to Colorado. Reasons why I moved reflect the typical phases in life that many people go through. I moved from Hawai'i because I had to grow up and learn to live independently; moved from Washington DC metro area when it came time to settle down and hated the lonely cold winters.

Finally, I left the San Francisco bay area due to the long commutes on ancient mass transit that frequently broke down, air pollution from the wildfires, astronomical housing costs, droughts due to water shortages, frequent earthquakes; in short it was not a great place to raise a family. Ultimately as life changes and circumstances dictate, moving is often necessary.

Sometimes you will find the need to move for cyber security jobs or to be closer to family and loved ones. Cyber security jobs are most plentiful in New York, Washington DC metro area, San Francisco bay area, Washington, Texas, and Colorado. However, outside of those areas it is a mixed bag. Some areas without a strong skilled workforce will tend to have more jobs than people and some companies will pay a premium for a person to move. Also consider where you are in life and where you want to be, lifestyle choices, family, friends, hobbies, and your plans for the future.

Know Yourself and Be Yourself

"Here's to the crazy ones, the misfits, the rebels, the troublemakers, the round pegs in the square holes ... the ones who see things differently -- they're not fond of rules, and they have no respect for the status quo. ... You can quote them, disagree with them, glorify, or vilify them, but the only thing you can't do is ignore them because they change things. ... They push the human race forward, and while some may see them as the crazy ones, we see genius, because the people who are crazy enough to think that they can change the world, are the ones who do."

-Steve Jobs

Working and building a career is always hard without guidance. One pitfall I fell into was not knowing who I was and what I wanted to do. Asian culture is full of restrictions and parents expect their children to be obedient. In the world of IT and cyber security, it is all too easy to get caught up trying to be who others want you to be and losing your own way. However, everyone first needs to know who they are. Because if you don't know who you are, it is harder to figure out which job is best for you. Also, you would forget what makes yourself special and different from everyone else.

Be Curious

"We pass through this world but once. Few tragedies can be more extensive than the stunting of life, few injustices deeper than the denial of an opportunity to strive or even to hope, by a limit imposed from without, but falsely identified as lying within."

-**Stephen Jay Gould**

Being curious is the key to open doors into cyber security. Ever wonder how do threat researchers find the latest security attacks; how do hackers hack, or how viruses are made? It starts with being curious, asking questions, getting answers, and next thing you know you are on a journey of discovery. You can do this by reading books, listening to podcasts, or even setting up a lab at home and trying it out. In cyber security, once the basics are learned, the advanced concepts beckon. For myself, I did not have that curiosity when I was young, and I am making up for it in my old age.

Networking

"You can make more friends in two months by becoming interested in other people than you can in two years by trying to get other people interested in you."

-Dale Carnegie

One of the keys to getting a job in cyber security is networking. Many people get discouraged applying for cyber security jobs when they see long job requirements for skills, experience, and certifications that seem impossible to get. One shortcut is that the people you meet at conferences and networking events are more likely to hire a person they know compared to someone they do not know.

Through networking events I met many amazing people and grew a very large global network. Networking can even be accomplished online through social media sites such as LinkedIn. Local events in the area are even better because you can meet and network with people closer to you.

I had a much easier time job hunting thanks to referrals and friends because it bypasses red tape and the many roadblocks.

Teach Yourself

"Never let formal education get in the way of your learning."

-Mark Twain

Like many other technology and cyber security professionals, most of what I know in technology and cyber security has been learned on my own. This became even more important when transitioning into cyber security. It comes down to whether you want to invest in yourself so that you can find a better job. I sure did. I even went back to school.

For many people who are unable to receive a traditional education or who do not have the time, there are many free classes and resources on the Internet. Also, if you join local groups, they will have training opportunities as well. Even better is to get virtualization software, load up free software, and practise at home. Practising, developing skills, and being able to demonstrate those skills will also help in the job hunt.

The hard part is that technology is constantly changing, forcing us to keep learning. During my life so far, I witnessed the changes first-hand. My family's first computer was the Atari 800XL, followed by the Apple II, and then the IBM 8088 4Mhz. In college, they still used mainframes and dumb terminals while the industry shifted to the client-server model. Even for operating systems, I started off with

Microsoft MS-DOS 3 then watched as Windows became the dominant non-Linux operating system. Video displays changed too, going from black and white, to four color CGA, to sixteen color EGA, to 256 color VGA, and to the millions of colors we enjoy today. Even network technologies changed.

In one of my first IT jobs, they used 4MB Token Ring and eventually upgraded to Ethernet. Slowly other futuristic technologies are becoming mainstream: Blockchain, AI, IoT, and more. As for cyber security professionals we need to be able to deal with the current technologies and the future ones as well because each one brings their own set of challenges.

Get Certified

"Anyone who stops learning is old, whether at twenty or eighty. Anyone who keeps learning stays young."

-Henry Ford

I have more than 20 IT and cyber security certifications that reflect my career history. Starting with A+ when I was starting out in IT, MCSE (Microsoft Certified Systems Engineer) when I was a systems administrator, CISSP (Certified Information Systems Security Professional) when I got started in cyber security, and

CCSP (Certified Cloud Security Professional) when I started working in cloud security.

The value of certifications has been controversial and debated for years but for me, their value is undeniable and have been essential when finding new jobs. For cyber security, Security+ is a great certification to start. Eventually, your goal should be the CISSP, the gold standard certification that is often required for many jobs.

Unfortunately for many people, certifications are a significant barrier to entry. They tend to have extremely high experience demands requiring verification while the exams are very expensive. Sometimes employers will cover the training and exam costs, others will not. Even when employers refused to pay, I did not let that stop me from taking and passing exams to get certified. There are many free classes and resources on the Internet that helped me. As a result, I have many certifications that reflect my long career.

One caveat to certifications is that due to the cost and time involved to prepare and take the exams, I highly recommend doing research to determine which certifications will best help with your career. A hacker would need different certifications compared to an incident responder. Another place to look are job descriptions that list the required specific certifications. Later on, when your career advances or if you decide to switch roles, you will probably need different certifications. So, it is best to plan ahead.

Attitude

"The greatest discovery of all time is that a person can change his future by merely changing his attitude."

- Oprah Winfrey

One trait that can set you apart when interviewing for cyber security jobs is having the right attitude. I have seen candidates try their very best to prove that they know everything and can do everything but failing to prove that they have the right attitude. A candidate has a better chance of landing a new job if they are a team player and can work well with others. Because if a person cannot work well with others, they probably will not be effective at the job. To me, a good attitude is more important than certifications or many years' experience.

Security is More Than Hacking and Incident Response

"As a young boy, I was taught in high school that hacking was cool."

-Kevin Mitnick

One of the greatest misconceptions of cyber security is that it is all about hacking and incident response. It seemed that way for me when I started in security. I had no insight to the other types of jobs out there. These include privacy, malware research, threat intelligence, cloud security, and more. My big advice is to get your feet wet and try different things in security. Many people such as I start out in cyber security doing security audits; but do not limit yourself. Cyber security jobs are as varied as the colors of the rainbow.

The big mistake I made when entering cyber security was taking the first job that came along. It is better to talk to people who have performed various cyber security roles to hear about what the jobs are like. There are also many online classes where you can learn and try out different things. Some areas will be more to your liking than others. The biggest mistake you can make is not taking control of your career letting others tell you which path to take based on their lives and not yours.

"One of the lessons that I grew up with was to always stay true to yourself and never let what somebody else says distract you from your goals."

-Michelle Obama

Sponsors and Mentors

"When you reach the top, you should remember to send the elevator back down for the others."

-Edith Piaf

When I started my career, I did not have a sponsor or a mentor. I never had guidance about options, career help, or direction. I just followed the system and accepted the path that was told to me. Today for career opportunities and advancement, it is critical to have a mentor, but more importantly a sponsor.

A mentor can help to give you advice and guide your career. A sponsor can advocate for you within the company and in the industry. My career would be very different today if I had one or both. Some people might be uncomfortable asking other people to be their mentor or sponsor. What would surprise you is how open people are to be a mentor or sponsor to you, just need to ask them. After you get started in cyber security and advance your career, it is important to give back and to help others. There is a need to pass the torch to others so they can succeed as well. In short, get a mentor and a sponsor, then become a mentor and a sponsor for others.

Develop Business and Communication Skills

"The way we communicate with others and with ourselves ultimately determines the quality of our lives."
-Anthony Robbins

Business and communication skills are critical when working in cyber security. I have met many individuals over the years who can build world class data centers, who know deep technical knowledge of concepts that are beyond me, and who are deeply sought after by the industry. Many of the same people did not have business skills and were unprepared when their organizations went bankrupt.

Others are unable to communicate effectively so they fail in job interviews or are unable to use the right method of communication when managing teams. Communication is what brings the world together and is a crucial skill that in many ways is more highly valued to organizations than technical skills. Business skills and understanding the organization can help people to work better and more efficiently.

No Title, No Problem

"Titles are of no value to posterity; the name of a man who has achieved great deeds imposes more respect than any or all epithets."

-**Voltaire**

We live in a world where titles are highly desired and sought after. Yet despite my 20+ years' experience and 20+ certifications, I do not have a fancy title such as CISO, VP, director, or even manager. Part of the reason was by choice, other times I did not feel worthy or confident of advancement. Yet I never let the lack of a title hold me back. I have done much to help others, recognize others, and to help those in need. And to me, the impact of helping others is worth more than any high-level title.

Take Care of Your Health

"To keep the body in good health is a duty, otherwise we shall not be able to keep our mind strong and clear."

-**Buddha**

Working in security will often involve working long hours that can take a toll on a person's mental and physical health. I have worked in jobs throughout my career that went past midnight dealing with incidents, fixing problems, or getting things done on time. Many jobs in cyber security lead to burnout and has been accelerated by the COVID-19 pandemic and declining global economy. It is important to know your limits, ask for help, and worst case say "No". Also, exercise, eat right, meditate, and sleep.

Chapter 7

Name: Nathaniel Schooler
Position: Principal Consultant
Company: The Influencer Marketing Company Ltd
Location: Croatia

My Journey into The Technology Industry

Like many people during the last recession I was out of work. I had been in the drinks industry my whole life. Whilst I loved free samples, the tangible products, the great people, and the social nature of the trade, I needed to learn about technology.

Something in my life had to change, I wasn't fulfilled and knew nothing about the ever-changing technology that now runs our lives. My memories of going to the Jobcentre to 'sign-on' remind me of why I am glad to be in the growing technology industry, especially now with remote working!

I have one fond memory of parking my Triumph Daytona motorcycle on the wide pavement outside Guildford Jobcentre. When I came out, I found a parking ticket on it. It was £60 and the 'Jobseekers Allowance' at the time was about £36.10 per week. That put my life into perspective. I wanted to give the traffic warden a piece of my mind, but he got away!

I remained positive, despite the clear difficulties that lay ahead in making enough money to eat and pay bills. Within a few weeks I set myself up as a freelance consultant.

Before social selling became a 'thing', I closed sales on Twitter for an award-winning microbrewery called 'Triple fff'. On another occasion, after one email I arranged a meeting with the head buyer from the largest restaurant and bar chain in the UK. The brewery was listed on their procurement list and shortly maxed out their production capacity.

I used LinkedIn to find leads for another fantastic client – a drinks brand design company. This was where I began learning more about marketing and branding. One of the designers taught me about the Johnnie Walker Whisky brand – the slogan "Keep on Walking" and the iconic progression over the last 200 years is well worth learning more about.

After some success as a freelancer using technology to sell, I remember speaking to a close friend of mine. He has owned an internet hosting business for over 20 years. He kept reminding me I needed an online business.

I eventually listened and started by building a website on WordPress and hosted it on his platform. It's funny looking back now; I remember sending him messages asking him for advice. After about three messages he said: - "Google is your friend!"

It took me a little while to work out what he meant and then it clicked. I could use Google and YouTube to learn about pretty much any topic on the planet and it would stop wasting his precious time. To begin with, I spent a considerable amount of time learning more about how to use social media for selling and then ended up learning more about branding from an associate. He had worked on substantial personal, luxury and household name brands, written speeches for Prime Ministers, and even launched Petronas into Formula 1.

I also taught myself how to write business articles, causing my associates and me much frustration, my current business associate Mike also suffers from my bad grammar too I might add!

Once I had learned to write in this way (despite my English teacher at school having told me continually that I would be cleaning toilets) – IBM hired me to write blogs. I was delighted; some technology and marketing industry giants like Seth Godin were even hired to write some of the blogs too.

This success led me to being a part of the IBM Futurist community. This is where I pushed the boundary of the basic knowledge I had of technology and sat at a round table with senior execs from IBM and other companies. The editor of Wired magazine was there too. We discussed the implications of AI on people's jobs.

Then fast forward a couple years, my wife and I separated and eventually I got a new girlfriend. Her ex-husband happened to be head of global architecture for a very large organisation. For some reason I ended up having considerable cyber security problems. Not receiving emails, problems with the internet crashing and other related issues, including my iPhone being hacked. That is when I discovered the need for cyber security.

My brother used to sell enterprise level cyber security for Cisco and other major players, but I found that dull. Until my girlfriend hired a security firm to look after her house, the networks, and devices, I was unaware of the need for things like the latest patches and started to recognise ways to manage the risk of snooping. Up to this point I was unaware of most things cyber related, until I watched that situation unfold… and started to get to know some experts in the industry.

A few months later, while working for one of our partner agencies, I had literally just interviewed one of the most influential people in cyber security within the UK for a big corporate client. After our interview I accepted a friend request from him and then almost immediately my website was hacked. It was dead within 5 seconds of me accepting his friend request. Facebook and most other social media sites are a minefield security-wise. This intruder found this easy and saw the opportunity to hack.

Once my website had been hacked, my interest in cyber security was born!

I interviewed Monique Morrow shortly afterwards, she's an ex Cisco CTO and asked her: - "Why do people do this sort of stuff?" She just replied: - "Hackers just hack…"

After this, I learnt quickly how to restore a website from a backup stored on the server and it only took me five minutes. Ok I confess, five minutes of deep panic and distress!

Since then I have become great friends with many great people within the cyber security space, including Chris Windley, Lisa Ventura, Tyler Cohen Wood (ex Cyber Security Chief of The US D.O.D.). They have taught me a lot about cyber. I have created content for Oracle, IBM and others around technology and I have also written content for Brother Printers on the security of printer networks.

Now I work to create market exposure, understanding and presence. We create, produce, distribute, and promote podcast interviews and associated media content for businesses and non-profits who want to amplify their messages, engage, and extend their audience.

The technology industry is interesting and without cyber security it is unstable. Over the years I have seen something of the threats that bad actors and hackers launch on a daily basis. When I visited IBM's

Wimbledon basement technology centre for the second time it was a real eye opener. You wouldn't believe how many people try to hack Wimbledon during the tournament!

It's incredible how disinformation and the bad actors can manipulate the mass population. I find it very worrying that the general population seems to be both separated from counter opinions and from the understanding of the other counter views.

We are in an exciting world and we are also in a rather precarious position, where one's reputation and livelihood can be affected by a hack or a loss of data, living in an extremely distracted society where people's behaviour and opinions are affected by what appears to be osmosis from sources that present themselves as 'truth.'

Physically and mentally we are burning ourselves out, we are damaging our posture, we are damaging our necks from cranking them over looking at our phones.

I am waiting for a truly harmonious day when we have a better relationship with our devices. One which is not led by teams of UX (user experience) programmers, but teams of psychologists who focus on assisting our day to day happiness. This I believe will reduce the technology addiction and enable us to be more human and caring towards one another.

Our online world is a connected and very segmented place. Our news feeds are all different and fed by our likes and dislikes; our lives are permanently affected on a deep emotional level by the technology that we in some cases sleep with and also by the very algorithms of the so called "free" services that we know and like and in most cases somehow now don't trust.

We now know we are the product; we know we are lambs to the slaughter, and we are still leaving the algorithms and the notifications to push us into a subconscious state of flux. We listen for the notifications, we submit ourselves to the hourly torture, minute by minute with no let-up or breaks in most cases. In my world I am fighting this by attempting to not access the internet until 10am every day and educating anyone that will listen to this approach.

Thanks for reading and please reach-out to me for further information on what I am doing at Cyber Security Valley; you can visit my website www.natschooler.com. I'm approaching 200 articles and there are also loads of great links to really informative podcasts. I'm happy to point you in the right direction if there is something in particular you would like to learn about.

Chapter 8

Name: Philip Winstanley
Job Title: Security Leadership
Company: AWS
Location: Dublin, Ireland

As a child, my mother sold me into Cyber Slavery ...

I was a happy child, being allowed to play outside, get fresh air and exercise. Then one day, my mother got a new job - as a Journalist.

But this wasn't your usual "local cat rescued from tree" journalism, oh no, my mother got a job reviewing computer games for Amiga Format, ST Format and other Computing magazines of the time (remember, the ones with floppy disks sellotaped to the front of them?).

So, for weeks at a time, I was made (forced!) to sit at home and play unreleased computer games whilst my mother watched on - profiting from my cyber slavery.

Eventually, I was rescued by puberty and wanting more freedom, but this period of my life cemented my passion for technology and computing and would ultimately lead me to the profession that I love, but we will get to that later.

As kids we all fantasise about the jobs we will do when we grow up, be it, astronaut, racing driver, princess, or giraffe breeder.

From a very young age, I had decided I was going to be a policeman, I was going to catch baddies and put them in prison just like my heroes in "The Bill" a TV Police show from the UK.

But I wasn't very athletic (Go sports! etc). I was quite shy, and eventually convinced myself I could never be a policeman and never do that kind of work because that's what "real men" do, and I was just some Ginger kid with asthma, so that put an end to that childhood dream.

There were always books at home, bookshelves lined with the weirdest and wonderful books on everything from astronomy to trashy sci-fi space operas. Learning and reading were huge parts of my childhood, my mother greatly encouraged it. And books were where I found my sanctuary.

So given this environment, I did the only thing I could do, I excelled academically in my earlier years of schooling, and up until my early teens, I tried very hard, getting top marks and grades.

Then something in me just lost interest in academic learning and cared more about connecting with people, with my tribe; I stopped trying, I rebelled against academia and I crashed in most of my high school exams getting poor grades.

What I did do though was start connecting with people online, on IRC Chat channels, on e-mail lists and early forums. I was learning and growing my knowledge, just not in the officially sanctioned ways. I'd found a bunch of other weirdos and geeks, techies, and sci-fi fans, just like me; I'd connected to my tribe. With them, I found a new lease of life and I was able to be my true self.

It was around this time that I came out as gay to my parents, which in hindsight, hiding that fact in those ten years probably caused a lot of the anxiety and problems I had with academia. Not surprisingly after just nine months in college, I dropped out, with just a few high school qualifications to my name including a C grade in GCSE IT.

So, I had no real qualifications, no real experience, and was still very-much discovering myself. I didn't know what to do with my life, but an opportunity came up and I couldn't say no. A friend worked at a computer games company and they needed someone junior to join their IT department. And when I say junior, I mean junior, it was paying £8,500 a year, but it was a job, and it was in computer games, and I would get to do IT – cool!

That job was great, it allowed me to experience a world of work, where all the grownups behaved like kids, they were creative and playful, my workplace had so much laughter and joy, passion and energy everywhere, from the artists and animators, to the sound effects guys and the developers, it was a magical environment for me at the fresh age of 17.

Whilst at the games company I started building software (I use that term very loosely, it was VBScript and a bit of HTML), and I loved it. I was being creative and innovative, my thoughts appeared on the screen, other people used my creations, the sensation was so rewarding, and I was hooked, I knew I wanted to be a programmer.

The only problem was, I didn't have a clue what I was doing, so I was regularly going out to Internet forums and email lists and asking questions (we didn't have Stack Overflow then!). Over time, I got better and learned from the generosity of others, and eventually, it was me answering other people's questions.

This got me spotted. I was pretty good at answering questions and helping developers out. I was using Microsoft technology sufficiently well, that I was asked, by Microsoft, along with a bunch of other people from around the world to go to Seattle for a secret meeting, where they showed us and asked us what we thought about this new technology they were thinking of, it was called .NET.

From that day on for about a decade, I was in the inner circle of the Microsoft Developer Division providing (free) feedback on tooling, technology, and ideas the development teams at Microsoft were producing. It was an amazing experience and I got to meet some awesome developers and technologists.

Whilst all that was going on, I was building code for the games company and talking to Microsoft about their super-secret plans. I got interested in meeting more people and building my tribe of technologists. This led me to start attending, speaking at, and then eventually running user-groups, technical communities, and conferences in and around the UK; I even wrote some chapters for technical books!

After a couple of years at the computer games company, and at the age of 20 I had decided I needed to make myself a professional developer and an opportunity came up for me to join a company that built consumer-facing websites for automotive manufacturers. I did that for a couple of years, met some inspirational people and learnt a lot about myself, but I had itchy feet and I wanted something else, but I wasn't sure what.

At this point, I set up my own company and decided I would give consulting and freelancing a go. I spent six years doing that, building software for lots of different organisations and sectors, creating and building. I loved everything that made it possible for me to do it , apart from the admin of running a company, and invoicing, and tax which I hated.

Then one day, I got a message out of the blue asking me if I would be interested in a role at Microsoft in the UK working with a team that advises developers in their customers how to write great code. It had been a dream to work for Microsoft since those early days of scripting and now it was a possibility, one I never imagined would happen, I interviewed and to my exhilaration got the job offer! So, at the age of 28, I joined Microsoft as an Application Development Manager.

And this is where my story takes a bit of a turn...

Not long after I started at Microsoft I was asked if I would be willing to get Security Clearance to work with the UK Government; I jumped at the chance. This was the start of my pivot into security.

The opportunity to work at the heart of Government with security-conscious departments and ministries gave me a broad and deep understanding of the challenges faced by both the public and private sectors when it comes to security practice and policies.

Using my knowledge of software development and computing, I was able to expand on that skill set and augment it with security thinking and culture to work across the public sector including Defence, Intelligence, National Security, Critical National Infrastructure and

Public Safety and also had the opportunity to engage with many private sector organisations in sectors including finance, utilities, communications, services and retail, delivering advice, guidance and consultancy from C-Suite executives down to engineers on the ground.

In parallel to my day job with Microsoft, I was encouraged by a colleague to sign up for the UK's Defence Intelligence - Joint Cyber Unit as a reservist to help combat threats to the National Security of the United Kingdom.

As you can imagine, I have quite a few stories I could tell about my work in all of those environments, what I witnessed and some of the horrors we combated and fought off, some of which I can talk about, and some of which I can only allude to.

Whilst at Microsoft I built up and developed its cybersecurity practice focused on software development teams; this meant rapidly expanding my knowledge of Secure Development practices, Threat Modelling and how software fits into the cyber security landscape.

All of the exposure I had with customers allowed me to identify the main gaps every organisation seemed to have, which came down to two areas – knowledge of the threats facing them and how to think about threats and practical experience in defending and attacking.

This led me to build a series of security offerings that Microsoft could deliver to its customers in a repeatable fashion including Threat Modelling Workshops which were delivered hundreds of times, and also, one of my favourite exercises building a Cybersecurity Wargames offering.

The Wargames were great fun to build and run. We set up two labs in the Microsoft Offices in the UK in rooms next door to each other. We would bring in a team of people from one of its customers, usually a mixture of security professionals, developers, testers, project managers and non-technical staff, and split them into two teams to have them play the role of either the defenders or attackers against simulated environments which represented real-world systems running in the cloud.

The best part of this was putting all the hardcore technical people on the blue team and the non-technical people on the red team, and then watching as the blue team got destroyed by its project managers and other non-technical staff, highlighting just how easy it is to break into systems with the right guidance (and we offered next to none). Out of the back of the wargames, customers returned to their companies and organisations inspired to improve their defences and make security a more central part of their planning.

This taught me that no amount of PowerPoint will ever be as effective as play and that it's great to humanise things and show non-technical members of teams their contributions are as valuable if not more so to the security discussions.

Being at Microsoft also allowed me to work in two other areas outside of my day job. The first was working to improve Diversity and Inclusion across our sector by being engaged with Microsoft's LGBT+ organization GLEAM. One of the huge problems with the technology space is the lack of diversity and one of the best ways you can help is by getting involved in employee resource groups, be they focused on gender, race, religion, parenting, or sexuality. Support combating conscious and unconscious bias within your workplace and join or start similar movements to ensure you can help make the world a more inclusive and diverse place!

The second area I was privileged to work was in combating Child Sexual Exploitation (CSE) and Child Sexual Abuse (CSA) through Microsoft's Digital Crimes Unit and the UK's National Crime Agency. It is a scary area to contemplate working in, but I wanted to make a difference. I took some courses run by specialists in the field to make sure I was ready for what I was facing and learnt about online predators, how they operate, their psychology and what tactics and techniques they deploy.

My focus on CSA/CSE led me to be approached by the UK's National Crime Agency and the Dark Web Threat Intelligence Unit to join them as a 'Special' in a consultative capacity, offering advice and guidance on technology and helping them further their strategy to combat child exploitation and other areas including narcotics, firearms, fraud, money laundering and other serious and organised crimes.

The work with the National Crime Agency was some of the most rewarding of my entire life; I cannot express how much respect and admiration I have for the teams working in environments like those such as the NCA and the huge impact they have on society with limited resources and difficult circumstances. Oh, and I got to be a Policeman after all!

In late 2018 an ex-colleague from Microsoft, now working at AWS asked me if I'd be interested in setting up a new Security function within AWS. I won't lie, I was so comfortable in my Microsoft role and career that it was a very difficult discussion to have with myself, but, I challenged myself to grow, to try something new, as I wanted to try working on the inside of an organization running the security function instead of telling others how to do it through consultancy as I had during my Microsoft career.

I'd not had a job interview in nearly eight years and was very nervous and suffering a huge amount from imposter syndrome, but I eventually agreed to an interview with AWS – what did I have to lose, all they could do was find out I didn't know anything about security and was just winging it…

Well, it turns out, they not only liked me but also wanted me to work for them. And so, began the next (and current) chapter of my life and the story I'm living.

In October 2018 I moved to Dublin, Ireland and started working at AWS where I was employee #1 for a new security team that was being spun up. Over the last couple of years, we've built out a global team of specialists and experts from every possible field of security to help us run and manage a 24/7 Security Operations function. I have been blessed to be surrounded by people smarter than me who want to share their knowledge and do the right thing.

AWS has provided me with an opportunity to build a Security function in a way that works, not a traditional Infosec environment, but a security function that is customer obsessed and pragmatic in its approach. We have worked on innovative ways driving comprehensive AppSec and Secure Development programs, delivered on Security Operations at an unimaginable scale and all whilst sticking to our values of diversity, inclusion, and trust-based vulnerability.

Speaking of diversity and inclusion, whilst at AWS I have also helped to run the LGBT+ network here, wonderfully called glamazon, and the network I've built here through the employee resource group has been amazingly supportive and passionate at championing LGBT+ causes. Together with a colleague we set up a coalition of other tech companies including Google, Facebook, Microsoft to collaborate on improving LGBT+ impact in Ireland.

One thing I've learnt from AWS is to relentlessly surround yourself with smart people, and don't be afraid to be the stupid one so you can learn from the best.

Some other magic also happened whilst in Ireland that never would have if I hadn't taken a chance on that new role; I met the most wonderful man, Junior, to whom I am now very happily married, something I never imagined would happen to me.

I still have no qualifications or formal education; I can't see myself getting any either and feel I'm plodding along quite happily without "going back to school" and that my learning style is not one of the classrooms but one of trying, failing, and learning.

To continue to "pay it forward" I have set up an initiative called secYOUrity to help security professionals find joy and happiness in their work through training, mentoring, and coaching.

Throughout my career, I have been presented with rewarding opportunities, all risky, and all outside my comfort zone, and am glad that I embraced them. Each time an opportunity came up, I said yes. Was it hard? Very. Did I make mistakes and mess up? Many times. Would I do it all over again? Absolutely.

I want to finish this ramble with a phrase that I learnt whilst at Microsoft, and it's a mantra I live by every day; try it yourself.

"Come as you are, do what you love".

Chapter 9

Name: Rory Innes
Job Title: Founder & CEO
Company: The Cyber Helpline
Location: York, UK

As soon as I walked into the interview, I was handed a piece of paper and asked to read it out loud. My first thought was, "This is one of those advanced tests to see how you perform under pressure. You know, like the ones they do at Google." Excited – and nervous - I started to read…

"Hi, my name is <first name> and I am calling from <name of large cash and carry chain>. Have you heard about our recent promotion?" Confused, I stopped and scanned the rest of the double-sided telephone script, clearly a telemarketing script for finding new customers. The interviewer realised I wasn't sure what this was about and said, "The marketing placement will be six months of you on the phone calling potential customers."

I went from being excited about putting my four years of business & marketing education into action, to thinking I might just have wasted four years of my life (apart from the time in the student union, obviously).

I carried on reading the script and completed the interview; role playing with the interviewer trying to get her to sign up and take advantage of the discount. An hour later I got a call from the university placement coordinator. I had been offered the job.

I let her know that this wasn't what I was hoping for from my Marketing Management degree placement in industry. I left out that this was mainly because: (a) I could already read, and (b) I had already mastered how to use a telephone, and (c) I could have got this job (for more than I was getting paid on the placement) without a degree.

She was furious that I wouldn't take the placement. Fewer than a quarter of students managed to get a paid placement and I was lucky to be one of the ones to be interviewed.

I loved marketing. I loved studying business. I knew it was for me. I simply couldn't sit back and give away my opportunity to learn how to do the job and get my career started. I wanted to see a marketing team in action, not be sitting in a call centre.

That decision not to take a terrible placement and take a risk on something better coming along changed the whole direction of my life and career. Taking a risk, thinking big and making sure I was making the right decision was a lesson that would do me well. It is also a lesson I would need to learn again 15 years later.

Information security services?

With two weeks to go before the deadline for having a placement, I got another interview. The pressure I was feeling having turned down a rare placement lifted. At least I had another shot.

This time it was for a small consultancy, called *dns*, who provided information security services and had just launched a Managed Security Services offering. On the one hand, it was great news that I still had a chance to get a placement. On the other hand, I had no idea what information security services were. I read the brief in a bit more detail and learned this was to do with computers.

Now it is important to point out here that I was never interested in computers. Like any other child in the 80s and early 90s, I loved playing computer games. I played Aladdin on the Sega Mega-Drive for three days straight after I got it for Christmas, but I was never interested in how they worked. The first time I accessed the internet was from the university computer lab when I logged on in September 2000. Computer security was pretty far from my mind (and my expertise).

I attended the interview at the company's office on Princes Street in Edinburgh. This time there were two interviewers – the Sales Director and the SOC Manager. For the next hour, I had a great discussion on marketing, what it is and how it could be relevant for a services company like *dns* (Services marketing had been a real focus for me during my degree and I had a basic grasp on the theory, but it turned out to be enough to make it sound like I knew what I was talking about).

In February 2003, my new career in marketing information security services began.

Fast growth – learning fast

dns became one of the fastest growing tech companies in the UK and eventually sold to the American MSSP, SecureWorks. The *dns* team, combined with VeriSigns previously acquired MSS business, formed the EMEA arm of SecureWorks to push it into becoming a global MSSP. Almost exactly 12 months later SecureWorks was acquired by Dell.

I'd gone from being on a student placement with a 20-person company to leading marketing, inside sales and sales operations across Europe, the Middle East and Africa for one of Dell's business. It was an amazing journey and one I will never forget.

In hindsight, *dns* was the perfect place to get started. They saw the student placement as a way to understand how marketing could help them grow. There were a lot of basic tasks (database cleaning, event logistics), but there was also the opportunity to create a marketing plan, meet clients and learn how the business worked. As the only marketing person, I was thrown in at the deep end and it was exactly what I had hoped for when I turned down my first placement offer.

The rough and the smooth of being a non-tech in tech

Something they don't teach you in a marketing degree is that technical people largely think you are an idiot because you studied marketing. For some of the deep techs, marketing was seen as a kind of toddler playgroup – messing with colours and layouts – and not something that was required. For a junior marketing person this is a tough environment. I was a million miles away from understanding the subject area, I was learning the ropes of my own field and a lot of people thought my area was surplus to requirements. An overhead that wasn't needed.

However, this challenging environment taught me four very valuable lessons:

1. **Executive buy-in is critical for something new** – the aim of *dns* was to grow fast and exit the business. The owner and management team identified they needed more clients, more brand equity and to be on the radar of potential buyers. This was a sales & marketing challenge, not an information security one. The Board were keen for me to succeed and helped pave the way.

2. **Educating the rest of the business on why you are here is important** – I knew I didn't understand information security, but what it took me a while to realise was that nobody else in

the business understood marketing. In fact, their understanding of what marketing was and what it can deliver was worse than my understanding of information security. I worked hard to educate the other teams on marketing and how it could help the business (we all had share options, so everyone had a vested interest in growth).

3. **The business didn't need another tech** – Successful businesses have people with a range of skills, from diverse backgrounds and with different experiences. The business was full of firewall consultants, security architects and SOC analysts – but what they didn't have was a marketing person who could help drive forward that function to help take the business as far as it could go. As soon as I realised that my skills, experience, and background were important my confidence grew, and I was more effective.

4. **There are too many IT people in IT** – when you have technical people leading IT departments what you get is more technology. In most cases in information security, more technology is not a good thing. The more clients I met the more I realised they were more interested in new technology than in doing the basics well. Commercial acumen – and risk management - was being overwritten by that instinctive drive

for technical people to be excited by new technology. I realised having a different view made me unique.

Crossing the Rubicon (for the first time)

Having an amazing first job that fulfils a lot of your career goals makes it extremely hard for subsequent roles to stack up. After three years at Dell, I decided it was time – after 11 years – to leave my student placement.

Dell was in a state of flux having just gone private and trying to change away from the view of the market. There were obviously great things ahead for SecureWorks, but I missed the challenge of taking something small and trying to grow it. This type of challenge just felt like a better fit for me.

Leaving Dell felt like a massive decision, but what I didn't know then was that I would make an even bigger decision three years later. I took a role that would completely change my focus and career path and put me where I am now. The role was to go and help a small risk consultancy (non-cyber) that sat within a merchant bank and build a cyber security practice. What made this business interesting is that it had both business and private clients.

It became clear to me really quickly that the private client area was extremely interesting. The business had a large number of ultra-high net worth individuals as clients, owned a super yacht marina and had acquired a Trust & Fiduciary business – this meant a pool of over a thousand extremely wealthy families internationally.

For anyone who doesn't have experience with these kinds of individuals or families, it is important to think of them as small businesses with huge assets. A typically wealthy family can have over 100 staff (think groundskeepers, pilots, yacht captains, drivers, personal assistants, accountants, security guards etc), can have dozens of properties and an office full of people looking after their finances, investments, and charities.

They also have a unique set of requirements. Privacy is often top of the list, but brand damage for them or their businesses can be a top priority too. There are often multiple generations of each family who have competing ideas about family values and what should be shared online.

Within months we received a call from one our client's lawyers saying that the client had been hacked and close to £1.5m had been stolen. We took our corporate incident response skills and went to work helping this family understand what happened and try to recover. Around six months later, the investigation led to the police making a series of arrests of the criminals throughout the UK.

We set about building a successful business doing incident response and proactive security for the rich and famous. The need to be able to communicate technical concepts very simply meant I was a great fit to act as a communication bridge between the individuals and our technical experts.

However, it also gave me direct exposure to the challenge facing people who face these types of issues, but don't have unlimited funds to throw at security experts.

Not enough is being done

I was surprised at first how hard it was to get police and the big technology platforms to help the individuals we were supporting. Even though I knew that the criminals never really got arrested, I had always just operated under the assumption that people were being helped when they fell victim to this type of crime. How wrong I was!

The support for victims of cybercrime in the UK - and those experiencing more general online security issues – at this point was dreadful (spoiler, it still is!). The police are under resourced, under skilled and focused on other areas; only really able to support if it was a high-profile case, a large amount of money had been lost or there was clear evidence that pointed to a criminal in the UK (although usually it takes all three).

More and more of the ordinary public were approaching us for help, but there was only so much we could help with on a pro bono basis. The sums of money these individuals where losing was much smaller – although significant for the individuals – and so it got reported to the police but almost never followed up.

I started researching this area. There were hundreds of thousands of victims in the UK every year losing tens of millions of pounds. The impact to those individuals and the economy was staggering. How come nobody was helping?

An 80-page call to action

In 2016, the National Cyber Security Strategy was released that would define how the UK would protect itself from cyber threats until 2021. I was eager to read it and see how the strategy and funding was going to tackle the problem.

I downloaded the document and read all 80 pages. I read it again to double check. Individuals - people like you and me – were mentioned once (page 26, section 4.7):

"*As citizens, employees, and consumers, we take practical steps to secure the assets we value in the physical world. In the virtual world, we must do the same. That means fulfilling our personal responsibility to take all reasonable steps to safeguard not only our hardware – our smart phones and other devices – but also the data, software and systems that afford us freedom, flexibility and convenience in our private and professional lives.*"

What?!

Our strategic approach to the general public is…that they are on their own!

I asked my dad what he would do to protect his hardware, software, systems, and data. His response – '*First I would google the difference between hardware and software!*'.

Lots of good things came out of the strategy, but almost all of it was focused on government departments and businesses. The strategy was literally to tell the public it was their responsibility to protect themselves!

Now, put a typical member of the public up against a cybercriminal, online scammer or obsessive cyberstalker and there is only going to be one winner. But we are asking them, the public, to magically develop cyber security skills and keep the cybercriminals out. There are so many things wrong with this I don't really know where to start.

Imagine the outcry if we said that about crimes in the physical world:

Q Don't want to get mugged? **A** Should have learned Karate.

Q Don't want to get burgled? **A** Should have taken personal responsibility and dug a moat.

I didn't – and still don't – get it.

The Cyber Helpline: Crossing the Rubicon (again)

I read a quote on social media recently that perfectly describes the thought process that led to me setting up The Cyber Helpline:

"I always wondered why someone didn't do something about that. Then I realised I am someone."

It just became really clear to me that the experience I had working with wealthy families put me in a good position to work out how to help everyone who needed it in the UK. I also knew that the people in cyber security do a lot of volunteering, a lot of fundraising and a lot of the businesses had really good Corporate Social Responsibility efforts. What was missing was a vehicle to focus the expertise and charitable focus back on the industry that we work in. As a result, The Cyber Helpline was born.

In early 2018 I left my job and put up a website offering free help to anyone in the UK who was a victim of cybercrime or had experienced something malicious online. I wanted to focus 100% on building this capability. The first person contacted us in May 2018. She had been a victim of a vishing scam (scam phone call) and had lost over £1,000. We talked her through her options and helped her deal with it.

As demand increased, we realised, like in the MSSP world, we needed a technology that could identify the issues and help us automate the more common issues to allow our volunteers to focus on the complex cases. We created an intelligent chatbot that launched in November 2018.

The custom built chatbot works 24/7, allows users to remain anonymous and can diagnose an individual's issue and connect them to immediate advice. Interestingly, to be able to identify known cyber security issues from plain English descriptions we treat each attack like a disease. We map out each aspect of the issue - like symptoms, recovery options, compromise techniques, unique markers etc. - and then we apply a scoring system to make a judgment on what the user is experiencing. Currently we have a 77% correct diagnosis rate, which is way higher than we expected.

The chatbot is a unique capability that allows us to scale. Scaling is the big challenge in the ability to provide effective support to the general public and something that other organisations haven't had an answer for to date.

Fast forward around two and a half years and we are now over 50 volunteers and a chatbot helping over 400 people a month – and growing fast. In our second year our case load increased 362% over year one. Four months into year three and we have already opened 37% more cases than the whole of year two!

The Cyber Helpline is really a movement by the UK information security community to step in and help fill the gap in support for victims. We take volunteer cyber security experts and connect them with victims who need help. We have built an incident response service for the general public that has the capability to scale to meet the huge demand in the UK and beyond.

What's next?

I have a strong sense that this is the area I will stay in for the rest of my career. I have realised I am extremely passionate about making cyber security expertise available to all. My focus right now is on individuals, but there is also a huge gap for small and medium sized businesses struggling to afford expert help when something goes wrong. Help for victims of crime should not be based on ability to pay.

The focus at The Cyber Helpline is to bring in enough funding to help us support more people (ideally everyone who needs it). We need to raise our brand awareness so victims throughout the UK know where we are when something goes wrong and we need to ensure we continue to safely scale and mature. We are building something new and we need to find elegant approaches in these areas to ensure we achieve our vision of a UK where the cybercriminals don't win.

Effectively supporting victims isn't going to be enough to reach this vision, however. There are two key areas we want to focus on: 1) Getting as many people into cyber security as needed; 2) Driving systemic change that solves some of the political, technological, legal and socio-cultural issues that drive and allow cybercrime to proliferate.

On the first, we hope The Cyber Helpline can provide a great way for people to gain valuable experience in the cyber-security industry, but also for experienced professionals to mentor people earlier in their careers. What we are also learning is that some time on the frontline has two major benefits for people in their cybersecurity careers: 1) It gives them expertise in responding to issues for individuals and not just businesses (useful when you are working on your organisation's human defences), and 2) Seeing the impact on individuals when data is lost or they suffer a breach can really give focus to the consequences of not getting security right when you are handling personal data.

On the second, we are in learning mode. We are gaining a unique insight into the threat landscape for individuals in the UK, why they end up being a target, the challenges they face and where they are being let down by the organisations that are there to support them with these issues. Soon we hope to use this learning to formulate some ideas on how things can improve. We will not be able to do it alone – the expertise needed is too varied and nuanced – but I think we can be a key part of the movement.

The cybercriminals can't continue to win.

I didn't mean to have a career in the cyber security industry, but now I am here I hope to do my bit to ensure the UK is one of the safest places to live and work online.

Chapter 10

Name: Tim Burnett BEng (hons), MSc, CISSP, AMBCS
Job Title: Security & Compliance Manager / Data Protection Officer
Company: Sykes Cottages Ltd
Location: Chester, UK

I didn't set out to work in information security (or cyber security, or data protection…). In fact, I didn't really want to work with computers at all. But back then, 30 or so years ago, these roles just didn't exist. Data security meant locking desk drawers and filing cabinets and making sure the office was locked up after everyone had gone home for the night.

Somehow, I stumbled into computing in the early 1990's and, as IT manager, did everything: networks, desktops with MS-DOS and Windows 3, servers running Netware 3.12 and dabbling with Linux for web and email servers. After a while, as IT systems became more complex, I started to specialise in networks before moving on to network security, information security and now, data protection and privacy.

This is the story of my career in cyber and information security to date. Whether a cautionary tale or an inspirational one, I hope you appreciate it.

I enjoyed tinkering with electronics and electrical things as a child, I didn't grow up with computers. I remember my cousins getting a Binatone computer game for Christmas one year that plugged into the TV and you could play tennis, squash and football on it – just blocks that moved up and down and a "ball" that bounced around the screen.

A bit later, a school friend bought a Sinclair ZX81 and we wasted hours typing in Basic programs from magazines which then, inevitably, failed to work or it crashed before we could run them. A little later came the rivalry between the Sinclair ZX Spectrum or Commodore 64. However, I never had one of my own; I was content soldering together the odd electronic kit to make disco lights which, nearly 40 years later, are stored in my garage, still work and get occasional use at children's parties! It wasn't until I went to university that I really started to do anything with computers. I hadn't realised that the course I had chosen – Electronic Systems Engineering at York – was so heavily computer-based. I chose the course because I had managed to get sponsorship from BT, and this was one of the three universities that their sponsored students went to (the others being Aston and Newcastle) and I liked the York campus.

It was here that I got my first real exposure to computing, programming and so on. There were others around me who had had loads of experience with computing and could programme all sorts of clever things; I battled my way through but really preferred to deal with discrete electronic components. Whilst at university, I bought my first computer: an Olivetti PC1; an 80188-based IBM PC clone with twin 3½" floppy discs with 512k RAM, running MS-DOS and text-based word processor, with a dot-matrix printer, on which I wrote up my final year assignments.

Whilst having a clear out a little some time ago, I found some notes from one of the management training courses that BT ran during the summer holidays where we had tried to write down what we did and did not like or want to do – it's somewhat ironic to look back on now and see that, under the "Do not like/want to work with" section I'd written down "computers" and "finance".

After graduating, my first job was as a "Process Manager" with BT in York, creating operational processes for a new (voice) network operating centre that BT were building in New South Wales, wargaming potential threats, working on ISO9000 quality management systems – and, somehow, I became responsible for the office computer system; a UNIX-based mini system with green screens that we used for word processing amongst other tasks.

The system had a remote access capability: a dial-up modem with dial-back on a predefined 'phone number. This was more to save the 'phone call costs than for security, although this was clearly enhanced as the system would only call you back on the number that was pre-configured for each user. You started a terminal emulator for that "green screen" view and dialled in with username and password; the system then called you back, you entered a second password and you were connected at the blistering speed of 2,400 bits/second, if the line was decent! This was only used for remote support or access by a very few people who might need out-of-hours access.

After a while, we moved to a local network with Novell Netware server and desktop PCs running MS Windows 3.0, which was the new BT standard; somehow, I ended up looking after this and helping others. Unfortunately, this was the time when BT was making some pretty big cuts to their numbers so, not long afterwards, I was made redundant.

After that, and with some cash in my pocket, I got a job as the network manager at Chichester College of Higher Education, a senior technician level role as part of the media services team.

This was when IT was part of the library and media services function and computers were a bit of a novelty – we had one Novell Netware 3.12 server on each of the two campuses which each had diskless workstations running MS Windows 3.0 on them. There were no unique user profiles or file storage; students simply stored their work on 3½" floppy disks which, inevitably, were thrown into the bottom of their bags to become battered and, often, unreadable.

My responsibilities included supporting the server – a Compaq i386 server with 32MB RAM – maintaining and running new network connections (10Mbit/s Ethernet "thin-net" with repeaters) and PCs, including a few stand-alone PCs in the library (to access data CDs) and in the college offices. At the time, none of these were networked; only the "computer rooms" had basic network functions to allow students to create and print documents, etc. on a networked printer.

I have memories of running networks on "thin-net" with crimped BNC connections and then fault finding using a time-domain reflectometer – a fancy name for a cable length finder which would tell you how far it was along the cable to a break. Very often a student would unplug the T-piece from their network card and plug the cable straight in, in the hopes that it would make their connection faster – instead, it broke the network. Other times the 50-ohm terminator would mysteriously disappear. "Thin-net" was notoriously unreliable; just moving a computer on a desk could break the link and shut down the whole network, disrupting any studies in the room until I or a colleague was found and able to fix the network.

During my tenure, we added a third computer room (another 30 PCs) on the Chichester campus with new-fangled (but much more reliable) twisted pair wiring from a hub. I was also responsible for specifying the requirements and design of the new telephone system. I added a 64kbit/s connection between the Chichester site and JANET – the Joint Academic Network – via Southampton University which gave us an Internet connection, and a 32kbit/s connection between the two campuses in Chichester and Bognor Regis so that this could be used on both sites. I built a web and email server using Slackware 2.0 Linux and Apache running on a pretty basic i368 PC and wrote the HTML code using a text editor (Notepad on Windows). The web site was mostly text with a very few basic graphics such as the college logo and a few photographs but, all of a sudden, in 1994, the college was online.

Looking back, I now realise that this was one of the very earliest web servers. I provided an early web browser (NCSA Mosaic), together with the then-common Gopher search facility to the student workstations using an IPX-to-IP proxy server called "Novix" running on the Netware server and networked up the offices so that a few staff could access email to the outside world. One of the lecturers was playing with an early release of MS Windows NT Server 3.5 and so this was used for the staff network (only around 10 machines initially). Without realising it, we had unintentionally deployed a 2-tier system, securing staff systems from students; something that would now be considered a basic minimum for ensuring the confidentiality of staff and administration systems!

Otherwise, at the time, there was very little in the way of cyber security – we ran a rudimentary anti-virus software on the endpoint PCs but that was about all. We hadn't considered the concept of attacking from the outside; in fact, the biggest threat to the systems was from students physically damaging the equipment through misuse, or a break-in and theft of the PCs as they were quite valuable.

Technicians at university colleges are not paid very much so, after a year, I moved to Aquascutum of London – a fashion retailer on Regent Street in London – to run the computer systems there. Once again, I was working with Novell Netware 3.12, along with a new HP9000 Unix system and an old (even then!) and temperamental Wang mainframe. Using my experiences from Chichester, I once again deployed an Internet connection, web and email server, and the trusty Novix application – this time more so that the whole company could access applications on the HP9000 via their Windows PCs, as Windows still did not, at that time, support TCP/IP as standard.

Life in London really didn't suit me, so I soon took the opportunity to move to Cirencester to join 3Com Remote Access Products – formerly Sonix – to join the team working on ISDN and WAN bridges and routers. Technology and computing were evolving rapidly by this time, and it was becoming hard to keep up with all of the changes, so I started to focus on networks. At that time, there were still many different network types and protocols.

Although TCP/IP was relatively well established, there was also a whole range of other, proprietary network types: Novell and Microsoft each had their own versions of IPX/SPX, Microsoft added NetBEUI (TCP/IP wasn't yet supported as standard on Microsoft Windows), then there were Banyan Vines, DECnet, Appletalk and so on. Building all of these into network routers meant that they were fairly complex in comparison with just running TCP/IP.

This was especially so on ISDN or analogue (modem) dial-up connections where call charges applied; we had to ensure that these would connect only when needed for data transfer and "spoof" the connection – pretend that it was still there when it wasn't – the rest of the time by building routing and bridging tables for the various protocols.

We still didn't have much in the way of security other than a rudimentary firewalling by blocking IP addresses and/or ports, although this was changing.

Sadly, 3Com closed the division and redundancy meant another move. I had a brief spell working for Crosfield Chemicals in Warrington, supporting their HP9000 and managing the upgrade of all of their desktop computer systems from Netware and Windows 95 to Windows NT 4.0 server and desktop as part of the "Y2k" compliance readiness, before moving to Rockliffe Computers (later

Ikon) in Runcorn as a network field engineer. My role included the design, deployment and support of Cisco and 3Com routers and firewalls as more companies developed Internet connections; some fixed line, although many were still ISDN dial-up.

Networking was made more complicated as a result of there being multiple different technologies and protocols. LANs were Ethernet, 100Mb, Gigabit, Token Ring (although dying out and being replaced – although doing so caused its own issues) and FDDI for campus networks. WANs were a mix of leased line, ISDN, X.25, frame relay and ATM. It also meant configuring support on devices for the mix of routed and non-routed networking technologies alongside TCP/IP such as IPX, DecNET, Appletalk – all of which are now long gone! Business Internet connections were becoming more prevalent and, with them, were firewalls such as the Cisco PIX that provided proper filtering.

I was also involved in supporting MS NT Server 4.0, in particular its use for forward and reverse proxy servers and email gateways, which started to offer more in the way of network filtering and security. What surprised me, however, was that other server engineers didn't understand the basics of networking. This was when I realised by how much computer systems had moved on, so that there were now specialists in different areas, such as messaging and desktop support, rather than being the general, "do everything" people.

My next role was as a pre-sales consultant with Cable & Wireless; a company that had seen the future and was moving rapidly away from providing voice telephony services to data. For years, voice minutes and non-geographical numbers (freephone and premium rate services) had proved to be very profitable, but it was obvious that data services would become more important.

My role was designing and costing wide-area network services using frame relay, ATM, and ISDN, including voice links and videoconferencing across these. Networks such as these were still, effectively, point-to-point with traffic being routed to central locations – such as between branch offices and head office. However, we were starting to see the emergence of IP networking over MPLS which allowed traffic to route directly between any point on the network with added features such as quality of service; a significant advantage for carrying voice calls. Remote offices could be connected using private ADSL connections or VPNs over Internet broadband links.

By this time, most systems were running TCP/IP and the other network protocols had died out. Very soon, the demand for the older network technologies – frame relay and ATM – were being replaced by MPLS and long-distance Ethernet. By now, there were more calls for better network security, but it was still very much network-level filtering on the router or sticking a firewall on the Internet connection. Very little, if any, monitoring was being done on the vast majority of these; they were pretty much put in as a "fit and forget" item; configured for the requirements of the day but never updated unless there was a significant change.

Sadly, C&W ran into some hard times and redundancy called again so, in 2004, I joined Atos (then Atos Origin) as a network consultant. Initially, the network team was very small but over time, through a period of growth and acquisitions, we became a pretty big team offering managed voice, network, and firewall services. I took over as manager of the technical security consulting team, providing operational security services (we provided a security manager and audit function) and network security designs.

I tried to develop managed security services yet, incredibly, it wasn't seen as a growth area. (Incidentally, I had also proposed that we push for and upsell on a more sustainable, environmentally-friendly computing model, using more efficient power supplies, data centre cooling, etc. but was laughed at, at the time; roll forwards a few years and this was a significant part of every bid that we responded to!)

My solution was to partner with a third-party cyber security company which had an existing managed security services offering, in order to sell a "white label" version of their services as our own. The idea was to demonstrate – at minimal risk to Atos – to senior management that there was a large demand for these services, at which time we would be able to build our own rather than be paying someone else to do it. After a significant battle, we did launch this service, although it was difficult to get our sales teams to understand and promote it. Once it was up and running, however, it was soon clear that there was a huge demand for proper, managed security services. Customers didn't have the resources to manage this themselves, but they knew that it was needed.

I moved internally to take on the role of UK CISO within the Security Directorate. This gave me an incredible opportunity to interact at a senior level across the operation of a large organisation and engage closely with peers around the world, as well as with both large private and public-sector organisations. I also worked with some highly respected and experienced security professionals across all aspects of security – from physical to data protection – and learnt a lot from them.

Here, much of my time was spent creating, publicising, and enforcing security policies as well as responding to and investigating security incidents. I spent some time looking into computer forensics, looking in detail at the contents of laptops and file types using tools such as Encase although, unless this is something you do every day, it is better left to the experts!

The most important thing I learnt was how to preserve the scene of an incident. This often meant coming into conflict with service managers whose role it was to keep everything running as it could mean disabling a particular service whilst investigating, such as traffic accident investigators will keep the road closed until they've gathered all of the evidence, much to the annoyance of road users. As the company became more global, with centralised rather than country-specific IT services, the need for individual country-specific security managers declined and I moved to help develop a new security consultancy practice offering niche and non-standard technology solutions.

By this time, the managed security services offering was more established but offering very limited services. It was apparent that these did not meet the needs of many of our customers: they were very restricted in what they could do, were inflexible, and took a long time to deploy. Our customers needed solutions which met their specific requirements and to be deployed quickly. Some wanted to use new, bleeding edge technologies; others wanted us to take on their existing products and manage them properly.

This didn't fit with a traditional, outsources IT managed services model that worked on volume (design once, sell many times). This is ideal for typical, corporate IT services such as Windows desktops, file and print services and standard IT such as email and databases but really doesn't work for information security, where the threats change rapidly and the perception of risk is different in every organisation.

In order to have the resources to offer these niche solutions, we also built a training academy for graduates and apprentices. It was clear that we couldn't recruit skilled people, so we built our own academy aligned with Derby University. Here, we found an amazing pool of young talent, many of whom had not done all that well at school yet were ambitious and keen to learn. We recruited on attitude and ability, rather than paper qualifications. We didn't always get it right and lost a few along the way who didn't fit, but the majority excelled. Unlike me, they had grown up with computers and never knew a time before them; the Internet, social media, online searches, etc. were all second nature.

Being taught by other, experienced cyber security consultants in the team, they soaked up the technology and, within a surprisingly short time, they were gaining certifications and working with minimal guidance on customer projects. I was able to share my experience from the management consultancy side to ensure that they understood the business focussed, risk-based approach.

Unfortunately, another corporate acquisition led to a restructuring which merged our team with the traditional managed services security team, and I ended up back in a security pre-sales role. As I had not been working closely with the technology every day, by now I lacked the pre-sales engineering knowledge. My interest was much more toward business risk, privacy, data protection and the then forthcoming GDPR legislation. This led to some very awkward discussions, such as being asked, "What technology can we sell which will make people GDPR compliant?" – it doesn't work like that.

This obsession with pushing a limited range of existing technology solutions and services onto customers is rather like pushing a square peg into a round hole – or rather, holes of a variety of shapes as no customer has the same problem to solve. For some reason, there was a refusal to use a "consultancy led selling" approach, whereby you first understand what the problem is that the customer would like you to solve and then come up with suitable solutions that are proportionate, relevant, etc.

Much of the time was spent chasing bid responses but, unless you have a good understanding of the client, you will never get very far and are probably only there as a pricing comparator and to make up the response numbers. I did find this incredibly frustrating and realised that, after 15 years in various roles, it was time to move on.

I joined Sykes Holiday Cottages as the Security & Compliance Manager and Data Protection Officer. I have found that almost all of my time is focussed on the DPO role and very little dealing with other cyber security aspects. The company is a travel agency, connecting customers with holiday cottages across the UK. Nearly all the applications that are used to achieve this (the database front end, search tools, website, etc.) are built in-house with a relatively large team of developers and business analysts.

I quickly identified that the main security concern was the database of personal data; not because any of it is particularly sensitive (and most could be found via other sources) but because of the volume and that it is all in one place. Although a lot of work had been done to ensure compliance with data protection legislation, there are still gaps – but then security is an ongoing process, not a one-off, tick box exercise. Data protection is based in law, rather than any technical standard, so the implementation of the legislation is still evolving and will continue as we see more court cases.

The world of compliance is a very different world to technical cyber security. The challenge is that there is no right or wrong answer. Being a data- and technology-driven company, I am still faced with the challenge of being asked to provide a technical solution to the compliance requirements – and there isn't one. Technology can be deployed to support the requirements – for example, identity and access controls to limit access to authorised people, or encryption to protect the contents of a database – but these are not defined anywhere in data protection legislation. The most common question I am asked is, "Can we do [xxx]?" to which there is rarely a simple yes/no answer.

Across my career, I have been fortunate to work with some very large, well-known companies including broadcasters, a global sporting event organiser, energy companies, finance companies, banks, manufacturers, distribution/logistics companies as well as government departments and defence. I have also worked with small, dynamic organisations. Outwardly, each has their own specific and unique set of requirements as they operate quite different businesses but, fundamentally, it all comes down to the same thing: protect the data from unauthorised access, change or deletion, whilst providing secure and uninhibited access to data for those who should have it; the C-I-A triad of confidentiality, integrity and availability.

The difference is the amount of risk that the company is prepared to accept, the likelihood of a breach and the value of the data being protected. The most important thing in any business is data and information – whether that is the intellectual property in a research and development organisation, the names and addresses of customers and employees, or the financial records of the company.

If information is so valuable, then protecting it is vital. Yet security is, all too often, still seen as an expensive overhead. In every aspect of information security people try to do it on the cheap. I've seen this especially in regard to data protection, where I am asked, "can we get away with not doing XXX; other companies aren't doing it." Companies will spend a fortune on advertising their products and having wonderful office environments, including installing door access systems, security lights and cameras – very tangible, physical aspects – yet will blanche at installing data security measures such as network monitoring, data encryption, user authentication, or data leakage prevention.

They would not dream of ignoring the financial services authority requirements, health and safety or tax laws, yet will ignore the legal requirements of data protection and e-privacy. The impact of a GDPR fine, compensation claims from affected data subjects and, worst of all, the reputational damage to the business could be huge. Human error is more likely to cause a breach than any technology – and the humans making those inadvertent mistakes are already inside your corporate network – yet there remains the perception that the damage will be caused by some outside hacker, so external barriers are built whilst employees have unfettered access to systems and information. An incorrectly addressed email with a sensitive attachment, dropped USB stick or a lost laptop is a far simpler data breach and can cause huge amounts of reputational damage to the organisation.

Cyber security used to be nothing more than making sure you had anti-virus and a firewall. As a result, it was seen as the responsibility of the computer or IT department and was something that was "done to" people, rather than being part of everyone's daily life, like locking the front door on leaving the house. This mindset is hard to change, especially at a board level where decisions on spending are made. The challenge for the security team is to get the balance right: weighing the risks against the vulnerabilities to offer a proportionate level of information security. It's also essential to speak the same language as the board member, which is why a risk-based approach works so well: you can apportion a financial cost to the risk, a cost to the mitigation and see where you get the most benefit.

If I were giving advice to a young, aspiring security professional, I would say: get across as many different aspects of security – not just technology – as possible and soak it all up like a sponge. Information security is all about business requirements and is very much about people first, then the business processes, and finally what technology can be used to help achieve the results.

It's much more evolution not a revolution – and the world is changing rapidly. Cyber and information security is a huge area and it's impossible to do it all.

Whilst you do need to decide on what area you want to focus on, don't feel that you have to stick there. Don't be afraid to move around to gain more knowledge and experience. Most importantly, build a network and, if possible, get a mentor. Working in security can be a lonely place and can give you a bad perspective on people – no-one will ever thank you; you'll only get complaints.

It seems that everyone is horrible, acts appallingly, is trying to break/attack you; is complaining and trying to sue you for a data breach, and so on. If you work in data forensics, some of the images, etc. you might come across can be very disturbing. Sometimes it feels personal; as DPO I will often receive an email saying, "You did [xxx] and it's disgraceful!" with a long-winded rant and I feel that it is a personal attack whereas, in fact, the "you" is "you, the company" not "you, Tim." They are often an aggrieved "keyboard warrior" who turns into a decent person as soon as they get a real person to talk to and realises that their concerns are being taken seriously.

For all of this, you need a support network to help keep that balance right and remind you that these are a truly tiny minority; the vast majority of people are decent, law-abiding, and just get on quietly! Looking back, I'm sure that there are things that I'd have done differently, but this is always easy in hindsight. There are aspects I love – including delivering training and public speaking – and things that are not so great, such as dealing with irate customers, or security incidents that (inevitably) happen at 9pm on a Friday and ruin the weekend. But overall, the role is never dull, and you get to understand all aspects of an organisation, and how businesses – and the people who run them – work.

Coming in November 2021 - The Varied Origins of the Cyber Men: Volume Two

"The Varied Origins of the Cyber Men: Volume Two" will be a compilation of inspiring stories and accounts from men in the cyber security and technology industries who are pioneers and leading the way in helping to protect the world from the growing cyber threat. It is hoped that this book will feature men in the cyber security industry from all over the world.

Those who are included and featured in the book will give their hints, tips, and advice to those who are looking to pursue a career in cyber security or technology or change their career path into cyber security or technology.

Submission Requirements

The Editor is looking for inspirational stories and accounts from men in the cyber security industry from all over the world who would like to be featured in the book, which will be released via Amazon Kindle Direct Publishing.

We are ideally looking to feature men who:
- Haven't had a linear path or journey into the cyber security and technology industries
- Entered the cyber security and technology industries from a non-technical background
- Started out in an entirely different industry to cyber security and technology
- Have overcome challenges or adversary to get to where they are today in cyber security or technology

We would love chapters to contain any relevant inspirational quotes, hints, and tips that you have which will encourage other men to enter the industry. And if you have had any animosity from any of your colleagues, male or female, we'd also love to know how you dealt with this.

We look forward to receiving your chapter submissions for volume two of "The Varied Origins of the Cyber Men".

Printed in Great Britain
by Amazon